ANGELS SPIRITS AND A 9 MM SCREW

ANGELS SPIRITS AND A 9 MM SCREW

LEGACY OF FAITH AND LOVE THROUGH FIVE GENERATIONS

Nanette Crapo

XULON PRESS ELITE

Xulon Press Elite
2301 Lucien Way #415
Maitland, FL 32751
407.339.4217
www.xulonpress.com

Printed in the United States of America.

ISBN-13: 978-1-6628-0283-6
Hardcover: 978-1-6628-0284-3
Ebook: 978-1-6628-0285-0

In loving memory of

DARRELL THOMAS CRAPO
1954–2015

Thank You, Heavenly Father, for Your longsuffering (patience) with the Doubting Thomas' of this world. Thank You, Jesus, for taking brother home. I miss him but I know I will see him again in Heaven! Thank You for loving us with such a profoundly passionate heart that You gave Your all for us. Worthy is the Sacrificial Lamb of God that took our place upon the Cross and paid our sin debt that we may have life eternal! Worthy Is Jesus, my Savior, my LORD, my God!
Nanette Crapo, 02/15/2019

"Then He said to Thomas, 'Put your finger here; see my hands.
Reach out your hand and put it into my side.
Stop doubting and believe.'"
__*John 20:27*__ (NIV)

"Jesus said to him, 'Thomas, because you have seen Me, you have believed.
Blessed are those who have not seen and yet have believed.'"
__John 20:29__ (NKJV)

DEDICATION

● ● ●

This book is dedicated to my mother, Mary Foust Crapo. Although I did not recognize the special kind of love she possessed within her heart as *fruit of the Spirit*, it was only because I did not know of such things until very recently. I have written of incidents concerning her that affected me deeply in a negative way as a child. However, as an adult, I have learned that what she said and did was blown out of proportion, twisted every which way possible, and turned against me by Satan to instill a sense of low self-worth in my child's mind. No matter what came against Momma, the devil could not keep her from passing to her children the legacy of her faith in, and her love for, Jesus Christ.

I am forever grateful for being blessed with a mother with *all* the *fruit of the Spirit* found in Galatians 5:22-23. Especially the fruit of the Spirit of *faith* and *love*, the *agape kind of love* of *Jesus*.

I also dedicate this book to my grandson, Christian Alexander Karamitsos, and to all the generations to come. They are our future. May they all be blessed with the *fruit of the Spirit* of *faith* in and *love* for Jesus Christ.

Nanette Crapo, December 4, 2019

> *"And now abide faith, hope, love, these three; but the greatest of these is love."*
> *1 Corinthians 13:13* (NKJV)

Table of Contents

⟡ ⟡ ⟡

PREFACE

●●●

I prayed in complete brokenness back in November of 2018 for God to put the pieces of me back together: spirit, heart, and soul. The enemy (Satan) immediately attacked me with thoughts of low self-worth that no one will read anything that I write because I am not qualified... I am nobody.

Then in January of 2019, while watching Christian television, God spoke to me harshly about the delay of starting *His book*! The Pastor looked right at me (through the television) and said that God told him to tell someone out there that was listening on T.V. to, *"Write that book!"* It was no coincidence that I just happened to be listening to Pastor John Grey on that particular day to hear those particular words. Those words were from God to me through him. Not to me only, of course; but I for one was watching and listening during the appointed timing of God.

That was the spark that lit the fire within my heart that prompted me to make a commitment and write this book with faith that it has been *"anointed by God"*; which that pastor also said, and I agreed with him! What was initially one book became two as the Spirit of God (Holy Spirit) directed me. It is very apparent to me that both books have been anointed. I acknowledge that I could not have written anything without the guidance of God's Holy Spirit. It is also very apparent to me that Heavenly Father has chosen and protected me since birth. "*Why?*" is the question. God has answered that question and so many more during the fifteen (15) months of intensive research and study in His Holy Word. I have learned much... I have much more to learn!

This book is a memoir of my early childhood years. It has a twofold purpose:

Firstly, it is to awaken those that do not know that Jesus loves them, and that God has a purpose for their lives. It is to awaken those that do not know Jesus to seek Him and discover God's plan(s) for them. I urge each of you to seek Jesus and find out why God has saved you time and again through miracles, not coincidences or lucky breaks... *miracles.*

Secondly, it is to awaken hearts as to the urgency of reaching out to our future generations and of enlightening them as to the gospel of Jesus Christ before they are lost forever to the darkness of this world. We must pray over our children as early as the womb for God's protection and teach them about the love of Jesus as soon as they leave the womb. It is imperative that we fill their hearts with love for, and faith in, Jesus Christ before the wicked one can harden those precious little hearts.

The devil can attack anyone, at any age and at any time. The younger our children are when Satan attacks them, the more chances he has of leading them astray into the darkness and away from the Light of the world, Jesus. We must nourish them and lead them to the Light, Love and Life of Jesus Christ. Without my introduction to Jesus at the tender age of three-and one-half (3 ½), and all the miracles of God's protection, I have no doubts that I would not have survived childhood nor the onslaught of evil against me in my adult years. That subject matter is covered in my book: AGAPE, LOVE CARRIED MY CROSS, PASSION IN

ACTION Crushing Curses, Healing Hearts, Saving Souls. Though two separate books they are very much intertwined. Together they make up my life's journey with Jesus and how I came to know and love His Holy Spirit that dwells within me.

I have also revealed some of the attacks of Satan against my children and the miracles that have saved them from certain death, or almost certain death, over and over again. Without God's army of angels surrounding us, we would not be here. I have referred to the spirit beings of God's angels as "*angels*" and the dark spirits of evil as "*entities*", "*shadow people*", and "*evil spirits*". I do not always refer to "*Holy Spirit*" as "*The Holy Spirit*", especially when speaking of Him as an individual because that is not His name. His very name identifies Him as Spirit... # *Holy Spirit*.

With agape in Jesus Christ,
Nanette Crapo 11/25/2019

> *"But Jesus said, 'Let the little children come to Me, and do not forbid them; for of such is the kingdom of heaven.'"*
>
> *Matthew 19:14* (NKJV)

INTRODUCTION

...

(Taken from Section 1, Chapter 3, Subchapter 2,
"*Discerning Sprits*")

There have been several occasions in my adult years when I have visually seen spirits manifest, both good and evil; especially during the night shift as a nurse in the intensive care unit. The supernatural realm surrounding us is full of both angels and demons. The age-old battle for our souls is ongoing!

On this particular night, I was at the bedside of a terminally ill patient that was at the end of life. I must not use "*he*" or "*she*" for I do not want to give their identity away. However, it is important that I mention my coworker on that fateful night, Patti T., as she was my only witness to the following incident, other than God Himself. Without a witness, I would be hesitant to mention such a nightmarish occurrence!

This night started as so many nights before, but this night ended like no other night before... or since! I was at the bedside the moment of their passing because I strongly believe no one should die alone. In the instant of the patient's passing from this world, I saw their face "screw up" or "shrivel up" ever so slightly! I began to wonder if I was imagining things! What I was witnessing was impossible!

The patient looked as if they were trying to get away from something! I had never witnessed such as that in all my years of nursing, and I do not wish to see such as that ever again!

I stood there for a few short seconds, perplexed and staring in disbelief. It was one of the most unnerving and frightening things I had ever witnessed to date; or so I thought. Only a few seconds passed when I saw "*them*"! "*Their*" movement caught my eye and as I looked up I was frozen in shocked horror. There was no way I could do anything to stop "*them*"! All I could do was pray! I backed out of that room very quickly! No way was I going to turn my back on "*them*"!

> "*They were swirling in unison around the ceiling! I found myself, wide awake, in the middle of a living nightmare!*"

(Taken from the journals of Nanette Crapo.)

I have referred to "*them*" as "*shadow people*" a few times because that is what most of us have heard about and can relate to; but these things were not and never had been "*people*". I am convinced that they were demons, entities from hell itself! They were very small, no more than a foot in length. They were dark, ghostly, see-through, fog-like evil spirits without visible facial features, arms or legs. I refer to them as evil because they had no light in them... not even the slightest flicker! It was as though they were clothed in hooded garments with the negative energy of darkness itself! The hairs on the back of my neck stood on end and my whole body became chilled to the marrow of my bones! I promise you this; I saw those evil spirits before the movie "*Ghost*" came out! The resemblance to the entities in that movie and what I saw was uncanny! I remember saying to myself, "*Someone else has seen those entities and made a movie about them*!"

Anyway, do not ask me how many I saw because I did not stay around to count them! They were swirling in unison at ceiling level over that patients bed... efforts to escape were in vain! I had seen enough! This was a look into the supernatural realm that I will never be able to erase from my memory! I implore you, do not let this happen to you or your children; or to anyone that you love! I will go as far as to say that I would not wish this upon anyone, period!

As I reached the nurses station, which was directly across from that patient's room, I quietly sat down in stunned disbelief... # in shock. I was too horrified to see any more! That was enough "*discerning of spirits*" to last me a lifetime. Previously to writing this book, I had only spoken about that manifestation twice; once that very night with my co-worker, Patti T., and again in April 2015 with my brother, Darrell Thomas Crapo... just weeks before his passing.

> "*Darrell Thomas Crapo is the brother that Grandpa Crapo was praying for so many years ago on the night of his birth; the night I was introduced to Jesus. I was only three-and-one-half years old, but the memory of that introduction remains as clear as it ever was. Of course, at that age I could not have known that both incidents would be so profoundly intertwined!*"

(Taken from the journals of Nanette Crapo.)

SECTION 1

CHILDREN OF GOD

...

"*For you created my inmost being; you knit me together in my mother's womb. I praise you because I am fearfully and wonderfully made; I know that full well.*"

Psalm 139:13-14 (NIV)

○ ○ ○

"But as many as received Him, to them He gave the right to become the children of GOD, to those who believe in His name;"

__John 1:12__ (NKJV)

"This is what the LORD says- your Redeemer, who formed you in the womb; 'I am the LORD, the Maker of all things'..."

__Isaiah 44:24__ (NIV)

○ ○ ○

CHAPTER 1

HEART OF INNOCENCE

. . .

> *"Train up a child in the way he should go; and when he is old, he will not depart from it."*

<u>Proverbs 22:6</u> (KJV)

As I began to jot down some of the many times that God has saved my life during my childhood, I began to remember more and more. Then I began to recognize them as miracles. This book should have been called *"miracles upon miracles"*! These miracles not only saved my life, time and again, but the lives of my children as well. But it is not about the miracles in themselves. It is about God's love, protection and purpose for my life, my children's lives and all the generations to come. It is about how He can intervene on one's behalf with miracles through objects, situations, other people, angels, His Holy Spirit, spirits, visions and dreams (*I could go on and on, but I will stop with dreams*) to bring His plans to fruition. I also discuss, in later chapters, some of the visions and dreams my children have reported to me that they have had. It seems to run in the family.

"And it shall come to pass afterward, that I will pour out my Spirit upon all flesh; and your sons and your daughters shall prophesy, your old men shall dream dreams, your young men shall see visions: ..."

Joel 2:28 (KJV)

The above was from the prophet Joel in The Old Testament of <u>The HOLY BIBLE</u>. The following was spoken by the Apostle Peter in The New Testament on the day of Pentecost as the Holy Spirit was poured out as Joel had prophesied.

"But this is that which was spoken by the prophet Joel; And it shall come to pass in the last days, saith God, I will pour out of my Spirit upon all flesh: and your sons and your daughters shall prophesy, and your young men shall see visions, and your old men shall dream dreams: And on my servants and on my handmaidens I will pour out in those days of my Spirit; and they shall prophesy;..."

Acts 2:16-18 (KJV)

In the case of my children and myself it has been mostly visions and dreams. God can communicate to anyone through visions and dreams. They are not unique to my family, I assure you. They are but examples of how God supernaturally and mysteriously communications with us. It would behoove us to pay attention and listen instead of listening to our own whining and crying. This I say to you lovingly from my own personal experiences. I pray that you, the reader, benefit from my experiences.

It is far, far better to be celebrating in victory with Jesus in His glorious light than throwing the same old pity party alone in a dark pit of gloom and doom from rejection and depression. Amen, and Amen to that! Of that I am living proof; for I should be dead, dead, long dead, as in not living or breathing in this corrupt and evil world. But because of Jesus and His unconditional and passionate love for me, I will be alive forever. What He sacrificed for me at the Cross, He did for the whole world. I do not deserve, nor do I have an exclusive on the passionate love of Jesus and God's promise of everlasting life in eternity. It is a gift to all that believe that Jesus is the Only Begotten Son of God. I, my children, and my grandchild believe. That victory over death, hell, and the grave through Jesus Christ is worth celebrating!

This leads me to a recurring dream I had over and over as a child of approximately eight years of age. This particular dream was instrumental in God's plan of salvation for my brother, Darrell Thomas Crapo, some fifty-five years later. All the glory to God! I know this dream was prophetic because God kept the memory of it alive in my heart. Sixty years have passed since the dream, but I still remember it vividly, as though it occurred only last week.

Faith in Jesus was instilled in me at a very early age. It has been a shield of protection that has lasted through my entire life. Faith is one of the *fruits of the Spirit: (Galatians 5:22-23)*

> **"But the fruit of the Spirit is love, joy, peace, longsuffering, gentleness, goodness, faith..."**

Galatians 5:22 (KJV) ;

as well as one of the *gifts of the Spirit: (1 Corinthians 12:7-11 and 12:28)*

> *"But the manifestation of the Spirit is given to each one for the profit of all: for to one is given the word of wisdom through the Spirit, to another the word of knowledge through the same Sprit, to another faith by the same Spirit,..."*

1 Corinthians 12:7-9 (NKJV)

I discuss both in later chapters. The point is, I truly believe I was blessed with a double portion of *faith*, which scripture supports as being a possibility. All I can tell you with all certainty is that I have never doubted for a half a nanosecond during my entire life (since the age of three-and-one-half) that Jesus was, is and always will be very much alive. *His presence, His essence is with me every day, every night, and everywhere I go.* It makes my heart extremely heavy to know some people do not have a personal relationship with Father God through His Son, Jesus; and do not realize that He is only a whispered breath away. You can invite Jesus into your heart, and He will never throw you away.

> *"All that the Father gives Me will come to Me, and the one who comes to Me I will by no means cast out."*

John 6:37 (NKJV)

-1-
THE CHALLENGE

Before I get started with stories of miracles; I challenge all you doubters out there to sit down in a quiet place and write down, or enter into your tablet, laptop, etc., all the times you were inexplicably saved from severe injury and / or death. There is an explanation. It's called a miracle; not luck, not chance, not coincidence, nor "*I was in the right or wrong place at the right or wrong time*"... a miracle.

> **"Miracle: An event that exceeds the known laws of nature and science. Usually an act of God done through human agents."**

(Dictionary – Concordance pg. 749 NKJV)

You too can feel the presence of God if you just stop long enough to take hold of Jesus' hand, the Son of God, and invite Him to come into your heart to be your LORD and Savior. All are welcome. All it takes is the faith of a child, no matter what your age.

I urge you to save your notes. You may have enough to write a book! The question to ask yourself is, *"Why was I spared?"* Search your heart. Jesus is calling to your heart; are you listening? God has a plan for your life, a purpose for your existence. God makes beautiful masterpieces out of shattered spirits, broken hearts, and wounded souls. *God is Light* and can dispel the darkest of darkness if you would only seek Him.

> **"This is the message which we have heard from Him and declare to you, that God is light and in Him is no darkness at all."**

1 John 1:5 (NKJV)

God did it for me and He loves you just as much. I am not special in any way. He loves us all equally and unconditionally and to Him we are all special. We are all His children.

> *"For God so loved the world, that He gave His Only Begotten Son, that whosoever believeth in Him should not perish, but have everlasting life."*

John 3:16 (KJV)

You can embrace Him or reject Him. If you reject Him *all will be darkness for eternity. Eternity... that's as forever as it gets!* God gives you a will to choose freely for yourself. He does not force His will upon you. God does not send anyone to the darkness of hell. Those that do not accept Jesus are condemning themselves. I urge you to do your homework! Research, study and actually read God's promises to you in His Living Word, <u>The HOLY BIBLE</u>, before you reject the only real "Truth"... His name is Jesus.

It is written that Jesus said:

> *"I am the Way, the Truth and the Life: no man cometh unto the Father but by Me."*

John 14:6 (KJV)

God knows our thoughts; He knows our hearts; He knows our anguish; He knows our deepest, darkest most intimate secret sins.

"*There is no darkness, nor shadow of death, where the workers of iniquity may hide themselves.*"

Job 34:22 *(KJV)*

Is your name in the *Book of Life*?

"*And whosoever was not found written in the Book of Life was cast into the lake of fire.*"

Revelation 20:15 (KJV)

"*And without controversy great is the mystery of godliness;*
God was manifested in the flesh,
Justified in the Spirit,
Seen by angels,
Preached among the Gentiles,
Believed on in the world,
Received up in glory."

1 Timothy 3:16 (NKJV)

-2-
HELD UNDER

"*Ye are of God, little children, and have overcome them; because greater is He that is in you, than he that is in the world*"

1 John 4:4 *(KJV)*

> **"And the LORD God formed man of the**
> **dust of the ground, and breathed into**
> **his nostrils the breath of life; and man**
> **became a living soul."**

Genesis 2:7 (KJV)

This story is the first attack brought against me by the devil (that I know of), and the first known miracle that saved me. Of course, the very first miracle of my life is my life itself. I am a miracle of God's creation... a child of God with His Breath in my lungs. You too are His creation; a unique and highly favored child of Father God, and do not let the devil tell you otherwise. After all, the devil has been exposed throughout The HOLY BIBLE as a deceiver, a liar and a thief! The devil wants to steal your very soul! Only God can create life, and only Jesus can assure you everlasting life; saving your very soul from the permanent darkness of hell!

> **"The thief does not come except to steal, to**
> **kill, and to destroy. I have come that they**
> **may have life, and that they may have it**
> **more abundantly."**

John 10:10 (NKJV)

Anyway, my family and I were enjoying an outing at a lake, and due to my age I was close by my mother's side. I was but an infant, barely able to sit. She became distracted and did not realize I was missing for several minutes. Although I do not know 100%, I am pretty certain that my mother cried out *"Jesus help me!";* a prayer I heard her cry out in times of trouble many times over the years.

"And whatever you ask in my name, that I
will do, that the Father may be glorified in
the Son. If you ask anything in my name,
I will do it."

John 14:13-14 (NKJV)

Her words still ring in my ears. Her battle cry became
my battle cry later in life when I needed Jesus the most;
and He did not fail me. On this occasion her cry alerted
everyone to help her search in the water for me. It took a
few more precious minutes to locate me. I was being held
under the water by a child larger than myself. He was sitting
on top of me! I had been held under at least three to four
minutes, maybe longer, before being rescued.

I know infants can hold their breath while under the
water and can be taught to swim before they can walk.
Remember though, someone larger than myself was sitting
on me which should have knocked the breath out of me or
at least made me cry; thus, getting water into my lungs. My
mother has said many times that it was a miracle that I did
not drown. My cousin, Phyllis J. Cusher, was a witness to
this miracle as the gathering was a family reunion. Although
only about four years old at the time, she heard from her
mother about this miracle while growing up. She and I
have reminisced about what we were told. Nevertheless, I
was held under long enough to drown! But by His Mighty
Power, His Mighty Breath in my lungs, He saved me to fulfil
the plans He has for me!

"For I know the thoughts that I think
toward you, says the LORD, thoughts of
peace and not of evil, to give you a future
and a hope."

Jeremiah 29:11 (NKJV)

It is Father God's decision as to when to call me home. When He does, I am ready, for I have an unction, a spiritual connection, a spiritual anointing, through His Holy Spirit:

> *"But ye have an unction from the Holy One, and ye know all things."*

1 John 2:20 (KJV)

Believers in Jesus Christ receive that unction through the Holy Spirit. Brothers and sisters in Christ, when you realize and utilize the awesomeness of the Holy Spirit within you, your whole world, your life, will forever be radically changed!

> *"Now we have received, not the spirit of the world, but the Spirit which is of God; that we might know the things that are freely given to us of God."*

1 Corinthians 2:12 (KJV)

> *"One God and Father of all, who is above all, and through all, and in you all."*

Ephesians 4:6 (KJV)

CHAPTER 2

FRUIT OF THE SPIRIT

...

"For you were once darkness, but now you are light in the Lord. Walk as children of light, (for the fruit of the Spirit is in all goodness, righteousness, and truth),"

Ephesians 5:8-9 (NKJV)

"But the fruit of the Spirit is love, joy, peace, longsuffering, gentleness, goodness, faith, meekness, temperance: against such there is no law."

Galatians 5:22-23 (KJV)

My dearest cousin, Phyllis J. Cusher, has agreed to be my witness as to the loving, compassionate heart that God gave me. She understands my heart better than anyone. As I researched for this book, I discovered the fruit of the Spirit which can define the character and the essence of one's very soul.
Nanette Crapo 02/25/2019

All who accept Jesus Christ as their LORD and Savior receive the *fruit of the Spirit* through God's Holy Spirit that comes to dwell within them! That in itself is beyond awesome and I am still blown away by the mystery of it all! This chapter discusses some of these gifts of the *fruit of the Spirit*. The first story speaks of the fruit of *love*. I do not know if it occurred before or after being "held under", as my age in one incident was very close to my age in the other. All the stories in this book are true stories. Some are from memory of stories that were told to me by my family and the rest are from my own memories which play like a movie in my mind.

-1-
A GENTLE HEART

> *"But the fruit of the Spirit is love, joy, peace, longsuffering, gentleness..."*
>
> **Galatians 5:22** (KJV)

Once as an infant in my stroller, I somehow got up against a hot oven door. I was asleep and yet the pain did not wake me up. By the time my mother found me and removed me from against the oven I had a very large blister on the back of one of my hands. According to Momma, I did not cry. She said I rarely cried. (Believe me, the emotional tears of rejection in later years have more than made up for the lack thereof.) I was a happy baby, always smiling and grew into an extremely timid child. Even when getting "spankings" I can remember crying because I had made Momma sad.

Now, I cannot and will not say that I did not feel pain because I did then as I do now! I distinctly remember using a cool washcloth after above mentioned "spankings"! I am saying that the emotional pain of rejection was and is far greater than any physical pain I have ever suffered. I can endure physical pain until it dissipates, which it always eventually does. It is the emotional pain that tends to set up permanent residence in my soul until it manifests into an actual physical pain that no human doctor or pill can cure.

I discovered in my adult years that the deeper one loves, the deeper the pain of not being loved in return will be, and the longer it will linger. Needless to say, the longer that kind of emotional pain lingers, the more it intensifies. Instead of dissipating over time, which would give one hope of recovery, it drags one down into a dark pit of depression. But I am getting ahead of myself. All of that is covered in my book, <u>AGAPE: LOVE CARRIED MY CROSS, PASSION IN ACTION, Crushing Curses, Healing Hearts, Saving Souls.</u>

For now, fast forward a few years. I would cry every time my little brother, Darrell Crapo, got a whipping. He was so small and frail that my heart went out to him. I even confessed to things I knew he had done and took the whipping in his place (sometimes... not very often). My compassionate heart made me protective of those weaker than myself, especially my little brother, Darrell. By the time he was around seven years old he would run around in a circle while getting a whipping. Momma would have a grip on his left arm as they went around and around, all the while he would be laughing at her! That made his whippings all the longer and harder! He was much braver than myself for being so much smaller. He never did learn to stop poking Momma Bear! Just the thought of that belt made me cry, but he laughed! Afterwards, he would go outside, hide behind the shrubs and cry. I know because I was there crying with him out of compassion. To see him cry always made me cry.

The memories of such times have been burned into my heart and into my memory. It still grieves me to remember, and I still "see" it like it happened only last week. I mentioned the above to Darrell during one of our last conversations before his passing and he said he didn't remember doing that; but he did remember the whippings... don't we all?

Let me interject here that I am not complaining about the way we were punished. I am sure we received what we deserved. I do not fault Momma in any way. Back in this time period I often heard her say, "*Spare the rod and spoil the child*". This is how my mother was raised and it was the only way she knew how to raise us. We do learn what we live... whether bad or good.

> **"Withhold not correction from the child: for if thou beatest him with the rod, he shall not die. Thou shalt beat him with the rod, and shalt deliver his soul from hell."**
>
> **Proverbs 23:13-14** (KJV)

Let me be very clear here that I am not condoning beating! However, I do condone correction. I can still hear Momma say, "*This hurts me more than it hurts you*". Only after having my own children did I understand those words that were spoken out of a mother's loving heart. It hurt her heart long after our physical pain was gone. Momma had a tender, giving, loving heart from God and it hurt her to correct us. She corrected us out of love; just as God does.

> **"My son, do not despise the Chastening of the LORD, Nor detest His correction; For whom the Lord loves He corrects, Just as a father the son in whom he delights."**

Proverbs 3:11-12 (NKJV)

There is a fine line between child abuse and correction. We can correct without physically attacking our children! For example: time outs, limited phone times, etc. The point is, we must set boundaries and correct unrighteous behavior in our children while they are young, to set their feet upon the narrow path of righteousness. Otherwise, they may take the more popular wide path of unrighteousness of the media and the inevitable peer pressure of their so-called friends. This may unknowingly open the door to evil; falling into the snare of the devil at an early age! Would you push them toward that door by letting them go and do whatever they please without protection? That definitely would not be in their best interest and that does not reflect your love for them! We must not turn a blind eye out of love nor out of ignorance and allow this to happen! We must not spoil our children and grandchildren to the point of losing their souls!

What I now know with a certainty, being a mother myself, is that Momma loved us very, very much! She just did not know how to express her love in words because love was not expressed in words to her as a child. (I have learned this in listening to her childhood stories.) I know Momma would have done anything within her power to protect her children. Whenever that protection was not within her power she never hesitated to call on the powerful name of Jesus! That was a truth I did learn from her, and I thank God for the faithful and loving example of a mother's unconditional love for Jesus.

"The only thing that counts is faith expressing itself through love."

Galatians 5:6 (NIV)

Rarely do I get angry, even now, and I do not hold a grudge. People, I do not boast! I tell you of the *fruit of the Spirit* that is strong within me. I am who I am by His grace and mercy; the way He intended me to be. But, to me, I am still that awkward, clumsy, overweight, shy and insecure child that has been betrayed and discarded by most of the important people in my life... the ones I loved.

I am learning that I am "fearfully and wonderfully made", and God loves me just the way I am.

"I will praise thee; for I am fearfully and wonderfully made; marvelous are thy works; and that my soul knoweth right well."

Psalm 139:14 (KJV)

I feel only sadness for lost soul's that did not get the foundation of faith and love for Jesus instilled in them as a child. We must give our little ones the foundation of faith in Jesus, as the Son of God, at an early age or we have failed them!

"The rod and rebuke give wisdom, But a child left to himself brings shame to his mother."

Proverbs 29:15 (NKJV)

I can forgive all day long, but because of my trusting heart I am incapable of understanding rejection and betrayal from others. Multiple betrayals sent me into a downward spiral of depression in my adult years which ate at my very soul, and it all started in my childhood. Only Jesus can take away that kind of pain, literally, and replace it with His unconditional love. Our children need the solid foundation of the knowledge that Jesus loves them to sustain them throughout their lifetime. That foundation of the certainty of His love saved me from the suicidal attempts of depression in my adult years. His agape, His love saved me from self-destruction.

I want my children and their children and all the generations to come to accept the love of Jesus and return it to Him. Without His love, we have no hope for a future. Deprived of His love we and our children are lost, and if we do not reveal His love to them... who will? And if one does not know about the mysteries of Jesus Christ found only in the pages of <u>The Holy Bible</u>, how then can one tell one's children that Jesus Christ is Love and the only way to Life eternal?

That pretty much covers love and now I will discuss faith. They go hand in hand. I truly believe in my heart that had I not received such a strong *"shield of faith"* (Ephesians 6:16) from Father God as a child, I would not have survived my adult years.

> *"above all, taking the shield of faith with which you will be able to quench all the fiery darts of the wicked one."*
>
> **<u>Ephesians 6:16</u>** (NKJV)

Without faith, I would not have survived the physical onslaught of the wickedness that I encountered in my years of backsliding! Amen!

> *"Thank You Abba, Father God, for giving me the fruit of the Spirit of love and faith and the Gift of the Spirit of faith! You knew before I was even born that I would be needing a double portion of faith to remain standing."*

Nanette Crapo 03/09/2019

I have been told that there is no such thing as different levels of faith. I have to disagree, for it is written:

of *great faith*...

> **"When Jesus heard these things, He marveled at him, and turned around and said to the crowd that followed Him, 'I say to you, I have not found such great faith, not even in Israel!'"**

Luke 7:9 (NKJV)

and of *little faith*...

> **"If then God so clothes the grass, which today is in the field and tomorrow is thrown into the oven, how much more will He clothe you, O you of little faith?"**

Luke 12:28 (NKJV)

"And He saith unto them, 'Why are ye fearful, O ye of little faith?'"

Matthew 8:26 (KJV)

Anyway, the good news is that whether one has great faith or little faith, both are covered equally by the Blood of the Lamb of GOD, the Blood of Jesus! And it is my belief that the *fruit of the Spirit* of love and faith make up the backbone of our inner strength that comes from Jesus.

"I can do all things through Christ Who strengthens me."

Philippians 4:13 (NKJV)

But if we do not recognize the *fruit of the Spirit* as the strengths from God that they are, we can easily become vulnerable and open to the exploitations of the evil schemes of the devil. Faith is everything! Without faith there is no hope! Without hope we have nothing!

"This hope we have as an anchor of the soul, both sure and steadfast, and which enters the Presence behind the veil, where the forerunner has entered for us, even Jesus, having become High Priest forever according to the order of Melchizedek."

Hebrew 6:19-20 (NKJV)

"Now faith is the substance of things hoped for, the evidence of things not seen."

Hebrews 11:1 (NKJV)

-2-
JESUS LOVES ME
The Bible And Grandpa Told Me So

"So then faith comes by hearing, and hearing by the word of God."

Romans 10:17 (NKJV)

"...That Christ may dwell in your hearts by faith; that ye, being rooted and grounded in love, ..."

Ephesians 3:17 (KJV)

"He never leaves me; He is within me! When a child knows Jesus is watching he or she wants to be good; seeks His approval through good behavior; and loves Him unconditionally as only a child can. Therein lies the faith of a child of God that will sustain one throughout a lifetime. I speak this from my own personal experience."
Nanette Crapo 03/10/2019

God chose me before I was born, gave me a free will to choose Him in return; which I did because of the faith in Jesus I received as a child. The whole point behind all the testimonies of miracles I'm about to share, is to stress the tremendous advantage our little ones will have if we reach them and teach them as early as possible. By the "terrible two's" they are already displaying defiant disobedience! It is up to us to nourish them, to feed them with His Word. I am living proof that His protection is real; as real as the devil's destruction.

> *"I will say of the LORD, He is my refuge and my fortress: my GOD; in Him will I trust."*
>
> *Psalm 91:2 (KJV)*

My earliest memories of conscious awareness, of existing, came upon me when I was barely more than an infant. I remember nothing before that time. This story and all that follow are firsthand memories from childhood to adulthood. It really is a weird feeling now as I think about it... like I just dropped from the sky in the middle of Grandpa Crapo's prayers for my mother and my brother, Darrell.

They were both fighting for their lives following his birth. Both were bleeding uncontrollably. My sister, Sharon, and I were being cared for by Grandma and Grandpa Crapo. Grandpa was praying out loud for Momma and Darrell while my sister and I were poking at each other and giggling. I would be willing to bet that Grandpa must have said a special prayer for us heathen children that were disrespecting prayer time. However, Grandpa continued praying without letting us interrupt him. I can imagine Holy Spirit was upon him; but when he was finished, he scolded us, and Grandma was crying!

My heart was broken! You've just got to understand that these were the most loving, hugging, and kissing people in my world! Grandpa gave such bear hugs that it felt like my ribs were going to crack, and sometimes he squeezed the breath right out of me. But I lived for and longed for those hugs. I never got hugs and kisses at home, really... never. That made me cherish their hugs and kisses all the more. I felt their love for me through those acts of affection. Making Grandma cry and Grandpa scold me was unbearable on my tender heart. I know my eyes were big as saucers. I was confused as to what I had done to make them so mad and so sad. Grandpa told us *"prayer time"* was time to talk to *"Baby Jesus"* and we made *"Baby Jesus cry"* because we were misbehaving during that prayer time. That's the very first time I ever heard about Baby Jesus and prayer time!

Wow! Not only did I make Grandpa sad and Grandma cry, but I made Baby Jesus cry too! Well, of course that in turn made me cry! Grandma picked me up and comforted me. I remember asking Grandma where Baby Jesus was because I loved babies and I wanted to hold Him. I often carried my sister around the house calling her, *"Baby"*... just saying; I loved babies.

Grandpa told me that I could not see Baby Jesus, but that He was there, and He sees everything I do and goes everywhere I go because He loves me. Well, there you have it! Jesus loves me because Grandpa told me so! Grandpa believed in Jesus and His daddy, God; and he even talked to them while I was watching, so of course, I also believed!

I believed and accepted that Jesus was (and is) real with the faith and love of a child, right then, right there and forever. And although I could not see Jesus, I did not question how that could be. I accepted Grandpa's words as truth, just as I now accept Father God's Word as Truth. I understood that Jesus loved me and no matter where I went, He went with me. I understood that whenever I talked He heard me. An unwavering faith and unconditional love for Jesus was forged in my heart that night. It remains an unbreakable bond of trust, faith and love between Jesus, the Son of God, and a three-and-a-half year old child named Nanette.

> **"Let the little children come to Me, and do not forbid them; for of such is the kingdom of God."**
>
> **Luke 18:16** (NKJV)

The story does not end there. Grandma closed the deal, so to speak. She asked me if I wanted to tell Baby Jesus that I was sorry for being bad so He would stop crying and be happy again. Of course, I did! So, for the first time in my life on this earth I prayed with coaching from my Grandma Crapo. From that moment forward, every second of every waking moment I have sensed His very presence. Even if I awaken in the middle of the night, I know He is with me and that always gives me comfort.

Jesus grew up with me, rather I grew up with Jesus. The night I met Him, He was a baby just like me. Then when I was five, He was five. When I was ten, He was ten, and so on. My mental image of His age was the same as my own age, thus we grew up together. Jesus was (and remains) my best friend. He calls me (us) His friends:

> **"Ye are my friends, if ye do whatsoever I command you."**
>
> **John 15:14** (KJV)

> **"This is my commandment, That ye love one another as I have loved you."**
>
> **John 15:12** (KJV)

When I was thirteen years old, I met my other best friend at school. Her name was Janet Chalk, now Sanders. She invited me to Sunday School where I met the grown-up Jesus. By the time I was fifteen I understood Jesus died to pay for my sins to give me eternal life with Him in heaven. I accepted Him as not only my Best Friend, but my LORD and Savior. I was baptized February 1967 and I still have the church bulletin announcement. (My sister, Sharon, found it in some of her old photos and recently gave it to me.) I now saw Jesus as a man, not a child or a teenager. He remains just as real to me today as the day I met Him at my grand-parent's house. The only difference is that I now see Jesus, my Savior (in my mind's eye), as the thirty-three year old Sacrificial Lamb of God Who died in my place on the Cross at Calvary. He has not aged as I have... He remains ageless.

> ***"Jesus Christ is the same yesterday, today, and forever."***
>
> ***Hebrews 13:8*** (NKJV)

Through the journey of this book, I understand that it is beyond my understanding to comprehend the depth of physical agony and emotional anguish that He suffered for you and me. What I do understand is that as much anguish as I carried in my **broken heart and shattered soul** for forty years (which I cover in my next book) is as nothing compared to what **was experienced by Jesus for us on the Cross.** Read, if you would, just the underlined bold type words by themselves as I have just noticed a message there. (Awesome!) I also understand that the depth of agape, the devotional and unconditional love He has for us, is also beyond my comprehension.

It is my prayer that every child receive faith in Jesus and believe in Him with an innocent heart full of unconditional love. I give all the glory to Father God for giving me the grandparents that watered the seeds of the *fruit of the Spirit* of *faith* and *love* in my heart and soul. I am convinced that it is because I was an innocent (yet not sinless) trusting child when I heard my grandfather's words that I was able to tenaciously hang on to my faith that Jesus loves me, even through the adult years of backsliding and heartache. As I mentioned in the previous story, faith and hope go hand in hand. Without faith, one does not have the substance to hope! It only takes faith the size of a tiny mustard seed.

> **"So Jesus said to them, 'Because of your unbelief, for assuredly, I say to you, if you have faith as a mustard seed, you will say to this mountain, 'Move from here to there,' and it will move; and nothing will be impossible for you."**

<u>Matthew 17:20</u> (NKJV)

Through faith do we receive His grace and mercy. Through Faith in Jesus are we saved by grace. All the glory is to Father God for His plan of salvation!

> **"For the law was given by Moses, but grace and truth came by Jesus Christ."**

<u>John 1:17</u> (KJV)

I know that I do not deserve this grace, but through my faith that Jesus Christ is the Son of GOD, I have received His grace. This grace cannot be bought or earned. It is a free gift to all that believe in His Holy Name (Jesus); and that He sacrificed Himself on the Cross to pay our sin debt. GOD loves us so much that He sent His only Begotten Son, Jesus Christ to save us! Jesus loves us so much that He endured untold suffering in our place to pay the price of death for our sins. Thank You Jesus, Yeshua!

Nanette Crapo 03/10/2019

"For by grace you have been saved through faith, and that not of yourselves; it is the gift of God..." Ephesians 3:8 (NKJV)

-3-
PEACEFUL SLEEP OF A CHILD

"Therefore, being justified by faith, we have peace with God through our LORD Jesus Christ:"

Romans 5:1 (KJV)

"I will both lay me down in peace, and sleep; for thou, LORD, only makest me dwell in safety."

Psalm 4:8 (KJV)

Part of this story I remember and part I do not because I was asleep. My mother told the story many times, thus all is in my memory. We still lived in Oklahoma and my brother, Darrell, was an infant in diapers. We moved to Texas when

I was five, so that would make me approximately four years old when the following miracle occurred.

Momma, my brother Darrell, my sister Sharon and I had just gotten home from where I do not remember; but I do remember we were in the green two toned '53 Buick. Daddy had purchased it just before Darrell was born and we brought Momma and him home from the hospital in it. Anyway, by the time we arrived at home, I was asleep in the back seat. Momma took baby brother into the house with sister, who was approximately six years old. Momma has said that she did not want to wake me and intended to come back and carry me into the house since I was asleep.

By the time she returned to the back porch, there was a pack of vicious dogs in the middle of the yard! They were between her and the detached garage where I was asleep in the car! She has said she was afraid I would wake up and try to run to the house. The dogs were fighting viciously and making quite a commotion! Although I had been sleeping peacefully, the noise eventually woke me up. I remember standing up and looking out the back window of the car and seeing the mean dogs. I remember being very frightened and then I saw Momma standing in the open doorway of the screened-in back porch. Her fears came to pass! I had one thought and one thought only... run to Momma!

This is when the miraculous happened! Just as I got out of the car and started running through the dogs toward Momma *they just disappeared*! I do not remember seeing them run off and had no idea where they might have gone as my eyes were locked on Momma (the way my eyes are locked on Jesus now). However, Momma has also said, *"they just disappeared"*!

> **"...In the mouth of two or three witnesses shall every word be established."**

2 Corinthians 13:1 (KJV)

My sister, Sharon, was also a witness. I waited for her to call me (she lives in Greece and calls once a week) and I asked her if she remembered when I was asleep in the car with dogs fighting in the yard blocking my way? She said she remembers (and I quote), "*They were there one minute and then they were just gone.*" She has given her permission for me to use her as my witness to this event. There you have it; three people witnessed those vicious dogs that could have, should have, torn me to shreds but *just disappeared*! No wonder Momma talked about it so much! She had a hard time wrapping her head around it. I am sure she cried out to Jesus for help! Even if she didn't have time or was too frightened to call upon His name... He was there.

> **"It shall come to pass**
> **That before they call, I will answer;"**

Isaiah 65:24 (NKJV)

Thank You Heavenly Father, for giving me a mother faithful to Jesus. And thank you for loving me so much that you gave your only Begotten Son to die in my place to pay my sin debt. I know that You chose me before I was formed in my mother's womb and that I am nothing without You! Thank You Jesus, Yeshua, for loving me so much that You suffered untold torment when You willingly gave Your life for mine... cleansing me with Your Precious Blood that I may have life everlasting in Your Holy presence! I thank You for being the Light in my world that keeps the darkness away.

Nanette Crapo 03/12/2019

> *"As long as I am in the world, I am the light
> of the world."*

> *John 9:5* (NKJV)

If you do not choose Jesus before your last breath, you will belong to the darkness forever. I just cannot comprehend my life without Jesus. His very presence has and always will be surrounding me, protecting me, and loving me unconditionally. I cannot imagine what the tremendous void of being without Jesus might be like. I thank God that I have no memories before meeting Jesus. One thing I am sure of; it would be total darkness in the absence of His radiantly blinding light of pure love! That would have been unbearable for me! I pray for those living in that empty void of darkness; that they may seek and find the love of God in the face of Jesus before it is too late.

> *"For it is the God who commanded light
> to shine out of darkness, who has shone in
> our hearts to give the light of the knowl-
> edge of the glory of God in the face of
> Jesus Christ."*

> *2 Corinthians 4:6* (NKJV)

-4-
LEGACY Of A MOTHER'S FAITH & LOVE

"And now abide faith, hope, love, these three; but the greatest of these is love."

1 Corinthians 13:13 (NKJV)

This is the perfect place to introduce you to my mother, Mary Foust Crapo. I would like to give testimony of the miracle of the legacy of her agape, her Jesus kind of unconditional love. Momma is a child of God. I say is because she is alive with Jesus in heaven right now. She had many lifelong friends. All who knew her loved her.

Although we did not have much in the way of material things, we had all we needed. I was fed, warm and dry and felt safe, but I did not "feel" loved. I only mention this because it is pertinent to my lifelong quest of searching for love, and longing to be loved. This was imparted to me by the devil as he exploited my feelings of low self-worth that left me feeling like a disappointment to my parents for not being "good enough".

It is extremely important that you, the reader, understand what I did not understand as a child. It was not intentional on the part of my mother to make me feel unloved. Momma was the most giving and loving person that I have ever known. How different life would have been had I realized that fact as a child. Momma expressed her love in actions and deeds. She just could not express it in hugs, kisses or words for reasons that were beyond my comprehension at the time. This left my vulnerable heart open to the lies of the devil that she did not love me.

I know now, being a mother myself, that she loved me very much and would have done anything in her power to protect me. She was raised by parents that did not display their feelings, their political beliefs or their religious beliefs. My parents did not share those things with us kids either. I could tell you that Momma loved Jesus, but I could not tell you what religious order she or my father claimed to be, if any at all. And I certainly could not tell you if they were democrats or republicans. I can tell you that she voted for whomever Daddy told her to vote for, without questions; setting the example for me of being submissive to one's husband. (We really do learn what we live.)

This lack of feeling loved as a child is one of the reasons that I am so very passionate about nurturing our little ones; not only in His Word, but with love. The kind of love that Jesus has for us all. I am saddened to tell you that I failed my own children when they were very young, as I became my mother by observation. I did not know how to express my love other than to protect them and try to make them feel loved with stuff. I literally missed their childhood years as I was at work more than I was at home. I have talked about my shortcomings with both my sons. They know that I love them both equally as I always have. They have both stated as adults that they understand, and they have both forgiven me for being gone all the time.

Momma befriended those less fortunate than ourselves. She always gifted our neighbors in need at Christmas with homemade cookies, pajamas, socks, jackets or whatever else they needed. The clothing items may have come from a garage sale (except for the socks). They would be washed and ironed (except for the socks) before being wrapped as gifts. The day after Christmas she would begin to restock her closet with gifts for the next Christmas. Her closet was strictly off limits for us kids.

Giving is a form of love in action. My baby brother, Max J. Crapo, has the charitable, giving love that Momma expressed; the agape (love) of Jesus for others. There is no debate as to who his role model was. I recall her continuing to provide basic needs for a widow and her son even after they moved several hundred miles away. Every Sunday afternoon she spent hours writing letters keeping in touch with everyone she knew from Texas, to California, to Oklahoma. She would have absolutely loved to have had a cell phone with "face time". She would have loved the instant connection with her many friends. I am very sure that the monthly bill would have been exorbitant!

Momma was always the "homeroom mother" in charge of the goodies at the various parties throughout the school year. She had four of us in school at one time and managed to be homeroom mother for all! As a grandmother, she continued this tradition for her firstborn grandson, Mark Curry. I do not know how she managed that, but she did! As the saying goes, she was the "glue" that held our family together. I grew up striving to fill her shoes and always felt as if I had fallen short.

On Friday, February 12, 1982, after getting dressed for Mark's Valentine party at school, she laid back down on her bed; whatever the reason we will never know. When she was discovered, she had a slight smile upon her serene face. She had the look of a child in peaceful sleep. In my heart, I know that she "fell asleep" and "woke up" in heaven. When you know that you know deep within your heart with such strong convictions... well, you just know!

Momma's peaceful smile was witnessed by seven (7) people that fateful morning, including my brother, Darrell Thomas Crapo. Seeds for the gospel of Jesus Christ were planted with that smile. It was a smile so innocent and serene that it will forever be her legacy to her children that death need not be feared if you have faith in Jesus Christ as your Savior. Amen! (Taken from the journals of Nanette Crapo)

I was a nurse for forty-three (43) years. Ninety-nine percent of that time was spent in intensive care, coronary care and emergency room settings. That being said, I have seen many things I wish I had not seen, for I cannot forget them. This includes many deaths. Some were so emotionally traumatic for me that I can see their faces and I remember several of their names to this day. However, never before, and I stress never before nor since, have I witnessed a peaceful smile upon anyone's face at the moment of death; except for Momma's smile on that Friday morning, February 12, 1982, two days before Valentine's Day. Although I miss her, I know I will see her again one day.

Had my mother lived, she would have surely had a very violent and painful death exactly one week later to the day. My father owned a pharmacy, and my mother was his cashier and all around do everything wife; from running errands to cooking his lunch and taking it to him (a distance of about 40 miles one way). One week later he was robbed in the middle of the day by unmasked, armed drug seekers.

> **"The righteous perisheth, and no man layeth it to heart: and merciful men are taken away, none considering that the righteous is taken away from the evil to come."**
>
> **_Isaiah 57:1_** (KJV)

Praise be to God that He called Momma home before the evil schemes of the devil could come to pass. God spared my mother untold pain and suffering. He took her home in the peaceful sleep of a child... a child of God.

Her peaceful smile told me that she was not afraid in the moment of her death. This then is her legacy that has been instilled into my heart:

- Faith in and love for Jesus,
- faith in His Promise of everlasting life,
- faith in the truth that death is not to be feared.

> *"O death, where is thy sting? O grave, where is thy victory?"*

> *1 Corinthians 15:55* (KJV)

> *"The sting of death is sin; and the strength of sin is the law. But thanks be to God, which giveth us the victory through our Lord Jesus Christ."*

> *1 Corinthians 15:56-57 (KJV)*

Thank You Jesus for taking my place on the Cross, for paying my sin debt and for giving me everlasting life. I cannot thank You enough with my words, but I can continually thank You with the agape (love) in my heart!
Nanette Crapo April 2019

> *Jesus said: "Most assuredly, I say to you, if anyone keeps My Word he shall never see death."*

> *John 8:51* (NKJV)

-5-
PEACE IN CHAOS

*"Be perfect, be of good comfort, be of one
mind, live in peace; and the God of love
and peace shall be with you."*

2 Corinthians 13:11 (KJV)

*"Peace I leave with you, my peace I give
unto you; not as the world giveth, give I
unto you. Let not your heart be troubled,
neither let it be afraid."*

John 14:27 (KJV)

The following story did not happen during my childhood; but I would like to include it here because God
brought it to my memory to illustrate peace of mind during
chaos. That is the kind of peace that only Jesus can provide.
However, even though I did not have time to utter a sound,
God's angles went to work and saved me with a multitude
of miracles.

*"It shall come to pass, that before they
call, I will answer; and while they are yet
speaking I will hear"*

Isaiah 65:24 (NKJV)

The majority of my career was on the evening / night
shift. The miracles in this story occurred on my way home
early one morning after twelve hours of night shift duty.

Even though I worked all night, and my drive home was a distance of fifty miles, I was not sleepy. I was very much awake admiring God's beautiful colors in nature. (I am definitely an outdoors person, being the happiest in my garden.) It was a clear morning in late fall and some of the oak trees had brilliant yellow and red leaves; fall foliage at its finest. The view was enough to keep me from becoming sleepy.

The last stretch of my journey was on a rural road; twisting and turning, up and down, around and through the hills and valleys. The foliage was so breathtaking to me that it distracted me from the dangerous curves of the road. The road did not have a shoulder to speak of, only about two feet of loose gravel. Just as I was within 800 yards of the entrance into my subdivision and just as I entered the last curve in the road... I lost control.

The chaos that followed is retold now from what an eyewitness told me and what I remember myself. I had not passed a single vehicle coming or going for 9 miles and I did not see the truck belonging to the "eyewitness". He was just there immediately after the roll over and stayed with me until the ambulance arrived; then he was simply gone. No one will ever convince me that he was not an angel.

He was not an illusion nor my imagination; he was there in the natural. (That does not eliminate him as coming from the supernatural.) I heard him telling the ambulance driver some of the details that I could not remember. When asked his name he simply said, *"Good Samaritan"*; at least that's what I heard him say before he disappeared. I lived in that small community for eleven years, where everyone knows everyone, and I never saw him nor his pickup again.

> **"For He shall give His angels charge over you, To keep you in all your ways."**

Psalm 91:11 (NKJV)

As I entered the last curve in the road, my right front tire left the pavement and hit the gravel. This brought my attention back to driving! In my panic, I overcorrected, jerked the steering wheel which immediately brought the right front tire back on to the pavement. However, the right rear tire hit the gravel which catapulted my car across the road at an angle of ninety degrees! It was as if I made a left hand turn going 50 miles per hour! By the time I hit the opposite side of the road, I had turned a one eighty and was facing the direction I had just come from!

I was fast approaching the ditch; not quite head on and not quite sideways. The ditch was very deep, and my car was very small. I became air born as I rolled through it and "flew" out the other side, tumbling in midair. Although it happened in the blink of an eye, it was in slow motion to me. It was surreal... supernatural! It was as though I was outside of time itself. I can understand how some people have reported having their lives flash before their eyes. There was time for that, and yet... there wasn't! For a brief period of time, I could not see anything, like my eyes were closed. I do not know if I had lost consciousness or if I closed my eyes from fright; but I heard everything, and I felt myself being tossed about like a ragdoll... in slow motion.

I heard the metal of my car crunching, ripping and tearing apart! I heard the windshield breaking! It seemed like it went on forever. In the natural, it was over in a few seconds. I wish I could explain it better than that, but it is, well, beyond my comprehension. Surreal, what else can I say? I am convinced that I was in a supernatural time zone under the protection of God's angels. You may think and say what you will, and I will not debate you. I know what I know because it happened to me.

Just as suddenly as I could not see, sight returned. My car came to a complete stop, right side up. My car was a standard, as in stick shift with clutch and all, yet even though my foot was off the clutch, the motor was running until I removed the keys from the ignition. How was it possible? Don't ask me! I thought to myself, "*Oh No! I broke it!*" Little did I know it was beyond broken, it was demolished!

Of course, I was scared nearly to death. Never before had I been in an auto accident of such magnitude. I have several bulging discs from my neck to my low back from years of lifting, transferring and turning patient's much larger than myself with the "help" of nurses much, much smaller than myself. So, I immediately began a mental self-assessment for any pain or discomfort. I felt nothing and for half a second I wondered if I was dead or perhaps paralyzed and unable to feel anything. I remember thinking that it will be just like this when my physical body dies, except instead of waking up in a cow pasture, I will open my eyes and see Jesus. Praise God!

It was at that very moment that God sent humor to me in the form of a very large cow. My only immediate concerns were that I might sustain such severe injuries that I might not be able to work ever again, and I was the breadwinner of the family. I once overheard my husband say "*I know where my bread is buttered*"... a fact he apparently forgot when the younger woman bewitched him. (Sorry, I digress.) If you want to know more, the sister book to this one continues with the adult years of my journey with Jesus. It's title is: AGAPE, LOVE CARRIED MY CROSS, PASSION IN ACTION, Crushing Cruses, Healing Hearts, Saving Souls.

Anyway, the first thing I recall seeing after the car finally came to a stop was a very large cow. I burst out laughing! All I could see was the white of her left eyeball as she ran past as fast as she could, trying to look at me without turning her head toward me! I was not laughing at the poor creature's fear; I was laughing because the cow was more frightened than I was. It sort of brought me back into the moment and put things in perspective. Peace returned to me in the middle of all the chaos. It would have been so quick and painless if God had taken me home right then. Here one second and in heaven the next, in the twinkling of an eye; peacefully falling asleep, like my mother.

Just as I was attempting to get out of my car (my door was jammed shut) the "Good Samaritan" was standing outside my window asking if I was alright. How he got there so quickly only God knows for sure. I say he was an angel sent by God Himself. Anyway, I told him that I was alright and kept trying to get out of my car. He told me to stay in the car until the paramedics arrived because I had not only rolled over, I had tumbled end over end! Angel or not, he was part of God's miracles activated to help me in my time of dire need.

Well, the ambulance arrived, and the driver's door was pried open. Before I knew it, I was strapped to a back board. I was so close to home and now I was going back to the hospital! Once there, I was subjected to an x-ray of my neck, a CT Scan of my head and a complete once over by the ER physician. Results...bulging discs (nothing new); a concussion with a bruise on the top of my head; a bruise on my right knee and a swollen knuckle. That's all I suffered! I believe with all my heart that the angels that God gave charge over me (Psalms 91:11) were in overdrive and overtime because the air bags had not even deployed! All the miracles that protected me were by His grace and mercy! To Him I give all the glory!

"But the very hairs of your head are all numbered. Do not fear therefore; you are of more value than many sparrows."

Luke 12:7 (NKJV)

Before closing this story, let me describe the car. The front and rear bumpers were ripped off, and along with other car parts, littered the pasture between the spot where I landed and the road. The top was crushed in and the windshield was shattered on the front passenger side only, sparing me! Both side mirrors had been ripped off and flung to places unknown. Both headlights and both taillights were shattered. The left side of my car from front to back was like an accordion, (thus the door was jammed). Needless to say, the car was totaled and like I said, the air bags had not even deployed. Instead of airbags, an army of angels completely surrounded me, as in 360 degrees, surrounded me! Even though I did not have time to call upon the name of Jesus, His peace was upon me in the middle of the wreckage, in the middle of the cow pasture, in the middle of the chaos.

"And I give them eternal life, and they shall never perish; neither shall anyone snatch them out of My hand."

"My Father, who has given them to Me, is greater than all; and no one is able to snatch them out of My Father's hand."

John 10:18-19 (NKJV)

-6-
INNOCENCE PROTECTED

"And a stranger they will not follow, but will flee from him: for they know not the voice of strangers."

<u>*John 10:5*</u> (KJV)

"I am Alpha and Omega, the Beginning and the End, says the LORD, who is, and who was, and who is to come, the Almighty."

<u>*Revelation 1:8*</u> (NKJV)

Once while on vacation in Oklahoma, I found myself alone on a rocky country road. I was eight or nine years old and doing one of my favorite things, rock hunting. Rocks have always fascinated me, and I am particular about which ones I collect, or I would have a room full. My keen eye searches for odd shapes and colors, but the really special ones are heart shaped. You might be surprised to realize how many natural heart shaped rocks God has made. I know for I have found many. God has never ceased to amaze me with His beauty in nature, which I appreciated even as a child.

As I was walking along that rocky road, alone, my head was down looking just ahead of my feet. I was lost in deep, intense concentration searching for my treasures and did not hear the car creeping up behind me until it was right beside me. A man (without any visible clothing on) stopped his car beside me and asked if I needed a ride somewhere. Having the fruit of meekness and gentleness prevented me from looking at him (for more than a glance), or talking to him, which protected me from untold horrors. Being the extremely meek, timid, shy child that I was, I quickly looked back at my feet without saying a single word. Then as quickly as I could I started walking back toward the farm-house where my mother was visiting with friends. The man in the car kept pace beside me and was now telling me to get into the car!

Even though nothing like that had ever happened to me before, I had a strong sense of fear and an urgent need to flee! So, flee I did! When I started running the car sped away and I was safe. At that age I was playing with my dolls and collecting rocks. Television programs were highly censored. I did not have the vaguest clue about such things as molestation, rape or even murder. There was absolutely no conception of such things in my innocent mind; yet I felt threatened and very afraid of the *stranger*. This was before the slogan, "*Danger! Stranger*!" and safety education. No doubt in my mind, Holy Spirit intervened for me and told me to run without me even realizing it for what it was... God's protection!

Once again the angels that have charge over me went into high gear. I ran faster than I was capable of in the natural. In fact, I have heard numerous times from my very own mother that although I was slow (physically, not mentally) I was graceful. She said it was beautiful to watch me swim (even though I came in last) and to watch me dive! But on this day, I had the urge to "flee" and I was faster than fast! My innocence and possibly even my life was protected.

> **"He will cover you with His feathers, and under His wings you will find refuge; His faithfulness will be your shield and rampart."**

Psalm 91:4 (NIV)

I believe with all my heart that God saved me over and over again so I could fulfill my destiny administering to the injured, sick and dying; first as a nurse, and now through prayers and visitations. Regardless of His reasons, which are beyond my comprehension, He saved me from a predator.

> *"It would be better for him if a millstone were hung around his neck, and he were thrown into the sea, than that he should offend one of these little ones."*

Luke 15:10 (NKJV)

> *"The LORD is my light and my salvation;*
> *Whom shall I fear?*
> *The LORD is the strength of my life;*
> *Of whom shall I be afraid?"*

Psalm 27:1 (NKJV)

CHAPTER 3

GIFTS OF THE SPIRIT

••••

"To one there is given through the Spirit a message of wisdom, to another a message of knowledge by means of the same Spirit, to another faith by the same Spirit, to another gifts of healing by the one Spirit, to another miraculous powers, to another prophecy, to another distinguishing between spirits, to another speaking in different tongues, and to still another the interpretation of tongues. All these are the work of one and the same Spirit, and He distributes them to each one, just as He determines."

1 Corinthians 12:8-11 (NIV)

Before I get into the *gifts of the Spirit*, I would like to tell my story about the night Holy Spirit intervened (again) on my behalf. Anyone that knows the Holy Spirit of God knows such things can and do happen.

"This is how we know that we live in Him and He in us; He has given us of His Spirit. And we have seen and testify that the Father hath sent His Son to be the Savior of the world."

1 John 4:13-14 (NIV)

One must accept Jesus with the faith of a child, even adults. We all begin as children in His Word and must learn by hearing and reading. When we believe by faith that He Is, we are forgiven of our sins. Only then do we receive His Holy Spirit and have direct access to Abba, Father God, and everlasting life.

Can you feel Jesus tugging at your heart? Do you feel alone and lonely in a crowded room? Do you feel empty deep inside yourself as though something or someone is missing in your life? Do you have a desire to have that emptiness, that void, filled with meaning? That is the space in your heart that is reserved for Jesus. He loves you just as you are! You have only to invite Him into your heart as your LORD and Savior. He will be the best friend you could ever hope for or ever imagine. Maybe you are asking yourself, *"How is that possible?"* It is possible because Jesus loves you so much that He suffered and died on the Cross in your place to give you the gift of everlasting life! His act of unequivocal agape (love), and the sheer agony that He suffered to express that love for you and me... is mind blowing! I do not comprehend it fully and maybe I never will; but I believe it with all my heart!

*"nor can they die anymore, for they are
equal to the angels and are sons of God,
being sons of the resurrection."*

Luke 20:36 (NKJV)

-1-
THE NIGHT HOLY SPIRIT SCREAMED

*"In the same way, the Spirit helps us in our
weakness. We do not know what we ought
to pray for, but the Spirit Himself intercedes for us through wordless groans."*

Romans 8:26 (NIV)

*"And He who searches our hearts knows
the mind of the Spirit, because the Spirit
intercedes for God's people in accordance
with the will of God."*

Romans 8:27 (NIV)

Very few people ever knew about the night Holy Spirit
screamed on my behalf in a life and death situation. There is
only my baby brother, Max J. Crapo, and myself left to bear
witness about what happened that night. Both my parents
and my brother Darrell were there but are no longer with
us on this earth. I myself am the only visual witness as to all
the events leading up to the screams, except for Holy Spirit
Himself; and He is my witness in heaven.

I was seventeen years old and my brother Max was nine. My sister, Sharon, was married by this time, thus she had moved out. The bedroom she and I shared still had both of the heavy solid wood twin beds situated side by side with walking space between them just as they were when she still lived there. If one were to stand in the doorway looking into my room, the foot of her bed was just inside against the left wall. My bed was to the right of hers with our dresser to the right of my bed. Going around the room, the wall that was past the dresser had a large double window with those old-fashioned metal blinds and no curtains at that particular time. There was a small shelf in front of the window full of trinkets and other things we collected over the years. The next wall at the foot of our beds had double closets with sliding doors. Just past the closets was the doorway to our room again, which was just off the foot of my sister's bed. That completes the panoramic view of our bedroom. The layout of the room is an important part of this story, so please bear with me.

With the bedroom door open I could see the bathroom sink as long as the bathroom door was also open. The hallway was in an L shape. If one were standing in my doorway and looking straight down the hallway, one would see the doorway to my parent's room. This was a small house, with short hallways. My two brothers shared a bedroom that was in between my parent's room and mine. Just across the hall from my brother's room and to the right of my doorway was the bathroom door. The hallway to the right of my door lead to either the front door through the living room or the back door through the kitchen. That is the complete layout, so on with the story.

My youngest brother, Max, was a sleepwalker and often passed by the bathroom in the dark. To solve that problem the bathroom light was left on all night long. However, this caused a problem for the light sleeper in the house... me. The light would shine directly into my eyes, so I was in the habit of closing my bedroom door. On this particular night, all was quiet, and everyone was fast asleep. Then everything changed when I woke up... rather when I was awakened by someone.

I was neither afraid nor startled even though I immediately saw him standing between the side of my bed and the window. Just as I was about the say, "*Max go back to bed*", something stopped me. I did not comprehend it at the time, but Holy Spirit was warning me that all was not well! It dawned on me, not of myself but by Holy Spirit, that my door was still closed, and it was very dark in my room. Doubt began to creep into my thoughts about this figure being my brother. He would not have closed the door behind himself, and I doubted he would just be standing there very still, looking at me. Then I noticed he was not being very still. He was moving very slowly; creeping toward me which made him sway ever so slightly as his weight was slowly shifting from foot to foot.

Fear gripped me! I froze! I could neither speak nor move. The devil had me in his snare of sheer terror! About that time, a car went by outside my window causing shadows from the blinds to dance across the walls and the ceiling. I could see through my barely opened eyes that he wore a long black coat. As the car was passing, he stood still. After the car had passed, he began to creep toward me again, ever so painstakingly slow! There definitely is something creepy and terrifyingly evil about someone creeping in the dark, especially someone that you do not know!

One more car passed then he was right up against my bed. I was absolutely petrified! I could barely breathe as my throat had all but closed in fear. Then he began to slowly lean over me and something deep within me told me that if I did nothing, I was going to die! I bear witness and testify that it was Holy Spirit that prompted me to flee or die!

What happened next may be controversial to all except me. I know what I know, and I know the scream did not come from me although it did come out of me. In other words, Holy Spirit screamed for me because I was incapable of doing such in my state of paralysis! It truly was not really a scream at all, but a deep, gut wrenching howl that could have raised the house off its foundation! In the natural, I am not capable of making such a spine chilling noise; especially at the volume in which it came forth out of my lungs! I could not even move until I heard that deep howling, moaning, screaming sound that scared both myself and the intruder in my room! I truly believe it frightened the devil himself, for he knew from Whom it came! It certainly was the wake-up call I needed to jolt me into action! As the horrendous sound was emitting out of my lungs, I closed my eyes as tightly as I could, grabbed my covers around my neck, and scooted myself to the top of my bed. I was sitting on the headboard with my back against the wall by the time my father reached my bedside! (The headboard railing was the size of a two by four board and I was literally sitting on top of it!)

Well, I am very happy to tell you that the intruder ran for his life! The table had been turned, so to speak. I felt him run into the foot of my bed as he rounded it to get to my door. By the time he opened my bedroom door a second scream / howl came forth from the depth of my being that was as long and loud as the first one. I cannot help but chuckle now to think that the intruder must have thought all the angels in heaven had been released upon him. Or perhaps, just perhaps, he thought all the demons of hell were chasing him? Little did he know he was surrounded by an army of God's angels the instant Holy Spirit sounded His battle cry. It is very possible that he was more terrified than I was. I like to think so.

> *"But to which of the angels has He ever said:*
>
> *'Sit at My right hand,*
> *Till I make Your enemies Your footstool'?*
> *Are they not all ministering spirits sent*
> *forth to minister for those who will inherit*
> *salvation?"*
>
> *__Hebrews 1:13-14__* (NKJV)

I could barely talk when my father reached my bedside, but I managed to say, *"There was a man hanging over me"*. Well, he told my mother later that I had a dream that a man was hanging over my bed, as in an old western movie. He also told me that all the doors were undisturbed and locked and that I just had a nightmare. My mother never bought that story and neither did I.

Here are the facts of that night:

- Momma said the first "scream" was muffled. My door was closed.
- She said the second "scream" was extremely loud. My door was now open.
- She said the "scream" sounded like a man, and she could not believe that I had made such a sound!
- I've tried to duplicate that sound... I cannot!
- My bed had been knocked toward my sister's bed.
- My father initially denied anyone was in my room but later...

- My father later said: "*You never thought there would be a man in your room either, but there was.* " (Aha! I knew it all along!)

I like to imagine God's mighty warrior, the Archangel Michael, appearing in my defense in the nanosecond it took to utter that first scream. I can imagine him leading the charge, running the evil man out of our house, chasing him down the street, and possibly even pushing him out of town with the tip of his mighty sword! I believe that poor soul fled in terror for his life! Who knows whether or not that mighty blast of God's trumpet (so to speak) scared him to the straight and narrow path of righteousness? Regardless, I bet he will never forget the sound of that scream as long as he lives! I know I never will! Now that I am out of danger, and the memory of that sound comes back to me, I can more fully appreciate how truly supernaturally awesome it was! My brother, Max, remembers that night and has agreed to be my witness. We are the only two left that was there that night.

I do not know if you have experienced anything like this before or not, but you too have access to the Spirit of God if you acknowledge Jesus Christ as the only Begotten Son of God and you accept Him, Jesus, as your Savior.

> **"If anyone acknowledges that Jesus is the Son of God, God lives in them and they in God."**
>
> **_1 John 4:15_** (NIV)

It still gives me chills to think of that night. Not only because Holy Spirit screamed for me but *because He can*. I know that Holy Spirit makes intercession for us in a language that only He and God can understand; but I tell you, He can scream for us too!

Sometimes God calmly says,

> ***"Be still, and know I am God."***
>
> ***Psalm 46:10*** (NKJV)

At other times Holy Spirit screams at you, or for you, to break your chains of fear and immobility. This is just another example of the mysterious ways of our Heavenly Father!

> ***"For through Him we both have access by one Spirit unto the Father."***
>
> ***Ephesians 2:18*** (KJV)

-2-
DISCERNING SPIRITS
"Shadow People"

"... to another discerning of spirits..."
"But one and the same Spirit works all these things, distributing to each one individually as He wills."

1 Corinthians 12:10-11 (NKJV)

"Thou shalt not be afraid of the terror by night; nor for the arrow that flieth by day; nor for the pestilence that walketh in the darkness..."

Psalm 91:5-6 (KJV)

The gift of distinguishing between spirits, good or evil, can be given to any believer by Holy Spirit as God wills. He gives this gift as we need it so we will be able to use it for God's purpose. In my case that purpose presented itself approximately twenty-five years after I saw the manifestation of dark spirits which I will discuss in this story. Even though the following occurred in my adult years, I include it in this book because it was instrumental in the saving of a soul. This story has a significant relationship with a recurring dream of my youth... so many years ago.

As a nurse, I have witnessed a death that was the polar opposite from my mother's peaceful passing. I witnessed a patient display a look of sheer terror upon their face at the moment of their death! I do not have to imagine what they "saw" because I saw the same thing! You may not be inclined to believe me, but I have the witness of Holy Spirit, and the witness of a coworker on that awful night! Her name is Patti T. Anyway, I would not advise that you ask God to let you "*discern*" or see the dark spirits that I saw. I for one do not think I could handle constantly seeing the kind of sheer darkness that I am going to tell you about. They are real, they are everywhere in the supernatural and they do not need spaceships! We cannot always see them, but believe me, they are terrifyingly real. I can now give my testimony, as a witness, not only that spirits are real but that the *gifts of the Spirit* are also a reality. They are from God... as needed, just as it is written in His Sovereign Word and God's Word is truth as He cannot lie!

It is written:

**"Look to Me, and be saved,
All you ends of the earth!**

For I am God, and there is no other.
I have sworn by Myself;
The word has gone out of My mouth in
righteousness,
And shall not return,
That to Me every knee shall bow,
Every tongue shall take an oath."

Isaiah 45:22-23 (NKJV)

There have been several occasions in my adult years when I have visually seen spirits manifest, both good and evil; especially during the night shift as a nurse in the intensive care unit. The supernatural realm surrounding us is full of both angels and demons. The age-old battle for our souls is ongoing!

On this particular night, I was at the bedside of a terminally ill patient that was at the end of life. I must not use "*he*" or "*she*" for I do not want to give their identity away. However, it is important that I mention my coworker on that fateful night, Patti T., as she was my only witness to the following incident, other than God Himself. Without a witness, I would be hesitant to mention such a nightmarish occurrence!

This night started as so many nights before, but this night ended like no other night before... or since! I was at the bedside the moment of their passing because I strongly believe no one should die alone. In the instant of the patient's passing from this world, I saw their face "screw up" or "shrivel up" ever so slightly! I began to wonder if I was imagining things! What I was witnessing was impossible! The patient looked as if they were trying to get away from something! I had never witnessed such as that in all my years of nursing, and I do not wish to see such as that ever again!

I stood there for a few short seconds, perplexed and staring in disbelief. It was one of the most unnerving and frightening things I had ever witnessed to date; or so I thought. Only a few seconds passed when I saw "*them*"! "*Their*" movement caught my eye and as I looked up I was frozen in shocked horror. There was no way I could do anything to stop "*them*"! All I could do was pray! I backed out of that room very quickly! No way was I going to turn my back on "*them*"!

"They were swirling in unison around the ceiling! I found myself, wide awake, in the middle of a living nightmare!"
(Taken from the journals of Nanette Crapo.)

I have referred to "*them*" as "*shadow people*" a few times because that is what most of us have heard about and can relate to; but these things were not and never had been "*people*". I am convinced that they were demons, entities from hell itself! They were very small, no more than a foot in length. They were dark, ghostly, see-through, fog-like evil spirits without visible facial features, arms or legs. I refer to them as evil because they had no light in them... not even the slightest flicker! It was as though they were clothed in hooded garments with the negative energy of darkness itself! The hairs on the back of my neck stood on end and my whole body became chilled to the marrow of my bones! I promise you this; I saw those evil spirits before the movie "*Ghost*" came out! The resemblance to the entities in that movie and what I saw was uncanny! I remember saying to myself, "*Someone else has seen those entities and made a movie about them!*"

Anyway, do not ask me how many I saw because I did not stay around to count them! They were swirling in unison at ceiling level over that patients bed... efforts to escape were in vain! I had seen enough! This was a look into the supernatural realm that I will never be able to erase from my memory! I implore you, do not let this happen to you or your children; or to anyone that you love! I will go as far as to say that I would not wish this upon anyone, period!

As I reached the nurses station, which was directly across from that patient's room, I quietly sat down without speaking, my eyes cast down toward the desk. I was definitely in shock, trying to process what I had just witnessed. I was horrified and did not dare look up to see more! That was enough "*discerning of spirits*" (1 Corinthians 12:10) to last me a lifetime. Previously to writing this book, I had only spoken about that manifestation twice; once that very night with my co-worker, Patti T., and again in April 2015 with my brother, Darrell Thomas Crapo... just weeks before his passing.

"*Darrell Thomas Crapo is the brother that Grandpa Crapo was praying for so many years ago on the night of his birth; the night I was introduced to Jesus. I was only three-and-one-half years old, but the memory of that introduction remains as clear as it ever was. Of course, at that age I could not have known that both incidents would be so profoundly intertwined!*"

(Taken from the journals of Nanette Crapo.)

Patti T. did not wait very long for me to speak. She looked at me and asked me in a whisper, "*Did you see that?*" She was in disbelief that I was in there and did not see anything! As I looked at her, I was still praying that I was just imagining things, but I knew better. I assure you, I am not known for vivid imaginations, hallucinations or fabrications of the truth. I cautiously asked her, "*See what?*" She said that she saw a "*black cloud floating around the ceiling!*" I use an explanation mark because she spoke with excitement although in a whispered excitement.

Oh my, I was not dreaming or seeing things after all! Of course, I knew I hadn't been as I never had before. But one has to question one's sanity when it is something so unbelievably nightmarish! I know in my heart that it was part of God's plan for me to be a witness and to have a witness as to what I saw. It was important to have confirmation that what I say I saw was what I did indeed see. What I witnessed (*shadow people*) may now be utilized as a weapon in the battle for lost souls through my testimony!

> **"For the weapons of our warfare are not carnal but mighty in God for pulling down strongholds, casting down arguments and every high thing that exalts itself against the knowledge of God, bringing every thought into captivity to the obedience of Christ,.."**
>
> **_2 Corinthians 10:4-5_** (NKJV)

I told her I did see "*them*" and that was why I backed out of the room! She looked strangely at me and asked, "*Them*?" From where she was sitting, in the light at the nurses station, it looked like one "*black cloud*" to her. I told her there were numerous very small individual shadowy, cloud-like entities swirling around together in that room A dark foggy mass of negative energy without definition of arms, legs or facial features! Sorry, that is the best I can describe them even though I can see them clearly in my mind's eye! They have been etched into my memory forever! I do not think that it matters much one way or the other what they looked like! Patti T. and I both agreed with what we saw! We both saw the same thing(s) from a different distance and from a different angle. And we both agreed that we had never seen such as that before!

We never spoke of "*them*" with each other again. However; I never forgot what I saw that night and I never will. The memory of it is counted as number one on my list of things I do not wish to see ever again! Unfortunately, there would be other discernments that have rivaled to be number one since that time and I shall never be able to un-see any of them! They are discussed in another book.

GOD has given me a sense of urgency to tell the world that time is running out; whether for you or someone you know. Jesus knows that you know for whom this story has been written! He has been calling you, tugging at your heart! So, here I am, giving my testimony as a witness, that the spiritual world of good and evil is very, very, very real. I cannot stress that enough! I pray you heed my testimony! For everyone out there that may be sitting on the fence about Jesus... please open your eyes! There are plenty of vacancies in Heaven and hell! The twinkling of an eye is not enough time to make a choice. I urge you, do not delay! You can accept Jesus anywhere, anytime. He sees you and He will hear you. He knows your heart. He is as close as the breath in your lungs!

Jesus is calling you to come as you are. All will be forgiven, and you will not have to worry about eternal darkness and creepy evil little shadow entities. I am prayerfully pleading to you... do not delay! If you see them, it will be too late to escape; too late to choose Jesus! I find that thought too devastatingly sorrowful for my heart and soul to bear!
Nanette Crapo April 19, 2019

"The night is far spent, the day is at hand.
Therefore, let us cast off the works
of darkness,
and let us put on the armor of light."

Romans 13:12 (NKJV)

-3-
PROPHETIC DREAMS

"... to another prophecy, to another dis-
tinguishing between spirits, to another
speaking in different kinds of tongues,
and to still another the interpretation
of tongues."

1 Corinthians 12:10 (NIV)

Please refer to the beginning of this chapter for the gifts of
the Spirit as listed in 1 Corinthians 12:8-11 as they are too
numerous and lengthy to list for this story. I urge you to review
the list and find your gifts.

For reasons known only to GOD, I had recurring
dreams about my brother, Darrell. The dreams occurred
over a period of about three years, not every night, but
enough to be stored in my memory until such time that
God called upon me to remember them. The dreams started
when I was about the age of eight and Darrell was about five.
As mentioned before, I felt very protective of him. I most
likely would have forgotten the dreams had they not left
me sad and upset. The dreams were prophetic, although I
was too young to know about such things. They were really

about the salvation of a lost soul that was drowning in a sea of sharks. It was about witnessing to my brother, before it was too late.

These dreams were not long ones. Our family was riding the ferry boat at Galveston, Texas. We were standing outside of our car looking over the railing. This is something we had done in real life many times. In the dreams my brother always fell overboard. The boat would not stop so I always jumped in after him. As I made my way over to him I would see sharks everywhere. I knew in my heart that if I could stay by him that he would not drown, and the sharks would not eat him. And somehow, I knew the sharks would not eat me either. Strange how I dreamt I was protected, and that protection extended to my brother if I could just stay close to him; strange but significant... prophetic.

Somehow, we were "breathing" under water or maybe we did not need to breath? I do not know because it was not an issue in the dreams. I would wake up with the memory of the sharks surrounding us and it always left me with a foreboding feeling. I remember feeling utterly devastated to think, "*what if the sharks had gotten him first?*"; "*what if I had not gotten there in time?*" The thought of never seeing him again always gave me anguish deep within my heart and always made me cry. Needless to say, I dreaded going to sleep.

I now think it strange that I felt like my presence could somehow protect him. I am understanding more and more that the presence of Holy Spirit within me gives me protection. This protection can be extended from one person to another through testimony and witnessing about the mysteries of the gospel of Jesus Christ should they accept Him. I have concluded that the #1 purpose of those dreams was to include them in my testimony as a witness to the unbelievers and the undecided doubting Thomas's of this world that they may believe in things not seen. It is my mission through these books to educate others that are as unschooled as I have been in the Word of God; thus, eradicating wrong believing and dispelling lies of the devil. I am to plant the seeds of the gospel of Jesus, but it is the decision of the listener to accept Him as their Savior... or not, for He has given us a free will.

I pray this book, my testimony, will reach those in need of the healing hand of Jesus Christ. I pray for hearts to be healed and souls to be saved as only He can do. It is up to every believer to enlighten others about the Light of Jesus and the darkness of the "sharks" of this world. We are to give them protection through His Word in The Holy Bible, known as *the sword of the Spirit,* which is part of *the armor of GOD* found in Ephesians 6:11-17.

> *"And take the helmet of salvation, and the sword of the Spirit, which is the word of God."*

Ephesians 6:17 (NKJV)

It has become clear to me that this is His will for my life, my calling, my mission. I am convinced that it is the only reason He repeatedly gave me those dreams and allowed me to "*discern*" "*shadow people*" long before the appointed time of need. Of this I am certain, without a *shadow* of a doubt.

> *"Put on the whole armor of God, that you may be able to stand against the wiles of the devil."*

Ephesians 6:11 (NKJV)

-4-
DOUBTING THOMAS

*"...Thomas, because thou hast seen me,
thou hast believed: blessed are they that
have not seen, and yet have believed."*

John 20:29 (KJV)

Of my other siblings, Darrell was the only one that I felt protective of, although I love them each and every one! He was the brother in the recurring dreams about the sharks at Galveston. I can still recall the feeling of agony and despair with heaviness in my heart over the possibility of losing him forever. I had insomnia because of those dreams. There was no way for me to know that is really was a prophetic nightmare in that I found out just weeks before my brother passed away that he was "undecided"!

I never thought to witness to him about Jesus on my prior visits. I just assumed he was saved; a misconception that a lot of us might have about our loved ones. Like our parents, we just did not openly discuss such things as salvation, religion and politics. We learned what we lived! I was shocked to find out on the very last visit that he was in doubt as to whether God was real or not! He was not saying he was an atheist; but he was definitely confused and undecided!

Darrell was very intellectually, scientifically and electronically minded. He was one of those nerds that could build and program computers before it was cool to do so; yet he was also very cool. He was easy going, quick witted, funny without the sarcasm, friendly, loyal and a devoted father. I could go on and on. Let me just say that everyone that met him loved him. He too, had a loving and compassionate heart.

As was with me, he did not know God's Word! He only knew what he had heard from friends and what he had heard on the television. How can one decide with such negative information found on TV? If we listen to the lies of the devil and allow ourselves to believe everything on TV, we are leaving ourselves defenseless. We are unknowingly inviting the darkness in while turning away the Light of the world which is Jesus Christ.

The devil is relentless and can make evil look good. Remember, the devil only steals, kills and destroys, (John 10:10) and he can destroy souls of unbelievers. So, I believe in my heart that God gave me (the shy introverted sister) a little shove out of my comfort zone to speak up about salvation. It truly was of God, because at the time I was lacking the knowledge to know how to witness for Christ! My heart was full of love for Jesus and my faith in Him was strong; however, I was ignorant of the mysteries of Jesus found in The Holy Bible.

The following is how it all went down: without a bible, without notes, without planning and without a clue in my head as to where my thoughts on the matter were going. More importantly, from Whom they were coming!

During that last visit with brother Darrell, I told him that Jesus has been with me since Grandpa told me about Him. Then I told him about the "*shadow people*" that I had seen one night at work. I had not planned to; it just sort of popped out of my mouth! However, it was not up to me. God was in control of it all! Before the memory of those dark shadowy entities even reached my thoughts and without realizing what I was saying, I started telling him how I know that heaven and hell are real.

> **"...do not worry about what to say or how**
> **to say it. At that time, you will be given**
> **what to say, for it will not be you speaking,**
> **but the Spirit of your Father speaking**
> **through you."**

Matthew 10:19-20 (NIV)

Think on that scripture for a few moments! Haven't you ever just blurted something out and asked yourself, "*Where did that come from?*" God had something that Darrell needed to hear, and He used me to tell him! That experience in itself is awesome and way beyond my understanding!

Anyway, I also reminded my brother of the smile on Momma's face and that I had never witnessed such as that before or since in my forty-three years of nursing. He sat there listening, I could tell he was processing this information, so I asked him if he knew the reason Jesus was crucified? He told me that Sharon, our sister, had been reading about that to him. She later told me that he had asked her to read it again and again in his last days. He was definitely seeking! Praise be to God!

> **"...for he that cometh to God must believe**
> **that He is, and that He is a rewarder of**
> **them that diligently seek Him."**

Hebrews 11:6 (KJV)

I am convinced that God had me see those dark entities to be a reliable firsthand witness as to their existence; not just to my brother, but to all who will listen. Our sister, Sharon, was the perfect person to explain to brother the plan of salvation for she is far more educated in God's

Word. All was set into motion long before any of us were even born!

> **"For my thoughts are not your thoughts, neither are your ways my ways, saith the LORD. For as the heavens are higher than the earth, so are my ways higher than your ways, and my thoughts than your thoughts."**

> **Isaiah 55:8-9** (KJV)

Thank You, Heavenly Father, for your wonderful and glorious ways! Thank You, Jesus, for paying the price for our sins with Your bruised, pierced and striped body; and Your Precious Life's Blood that was spilled at Calvary!

> **"you were bought at a price."**

> **1 Corinthians 6:20** (NIV)

After I told him about the dark cloud of "*shadow people*", for lack of a better description, we both just sat there for a few moments in awkward silence. To break that silence, I told him another story. It was about another patient I once had that embraced imminent death with peace. She, the patient, called her family to her bedside and told them that her time had come and not to be sad for her. She said her childhood pastor and her mother were there to take her home to Jesus. She said she could see them standing at the foot of her bed. Within five minutes of her family leaving her bedside she said, "*I'm going to sleep now.*" It was about 4:00 pm in the evening and she did just as she said. She "*fell asleep*" here on earth and there is no doubt in my mind that she opened her eyes in heaven; just like our mother did. Even though she did not have a smile as my mother did, she did look very peaceful, nonetheless! She never expressed fear of death, she embraced it. That is the peace Jesus gives believers!

> **"For if we believe that Jesus died and rose again, even so God will bring with Him those who sleep in Jesus."**
>
> **<u>1 Thessalonians 4:14</u>** (NKJV)

After another long pause, my brother said, "*I have never heard of anyone seeing the shadow people... except on a radio talk show*". (So that is what he was mulling over in his silence... the *shadow people*!) I told him that they *are* very real, that I had seen them only once in my life and that I prayed to never see them again! I told him it was not something I went around talking about, but rather it was something that I had suppressed in the depth of my memory... until our visit.

I was praying he would not forget about that which I had no intention of telling him in the first place... "shadow people". (From the journals of Nanette Crapo)

Next, I told him some stories about successfully resuscitated patients; about their descriptions of seeing "*the Light*". I said to him, "*Jesus is Light... go to the Light, go to Jesus!*" At that time, I did not know Scripture says, "*God is light" (1 John 1:5),* much to my shame!

> **"This then is the message which we have heard of Him, and declare unto you, that**

GOD is Light, and in Him is no darkness at all."

1 John 1:5 (KJV)

So why did I say it? Here again, this knowledge was not of me but of the Spirit of God within me. There is no other explanation that will convince me otherwise. And... it is written:

"But whatever is given you in that hour, speak that; for it is not you who speak, but the Holy Spirit."

Mark 13:11 (NKJV)

After that mind blowing experience, we both fell into another awkward silence. My heart was breaking, and I did not know what to say or do to convince him that Jesus is real and does not need a spaceship. That is what he was hearing on the television during my visit! An insinuation that there is no God was made with the statement that aliens came in spaceships and were mistaken for gods. That program is what prompted me to open my mouth and speak about Jesus. I pray for those nonbelievers on television that are leading others to hell out of ignorance of God's Word! I pray their eyes, and the eyes of those they have led astray, are opened to the Truth of Jesus Christ! Amen!

Darrell finally spoke, breaking the silence. What he said gave me hope that he was processing this new information with much deep thought and consideration of the possibilities of the reality of the unseen existence of Jesus Christ.

"I don't know where we go when we die,

<u>*but I know we are energy and energy will never stop.*</u>
<u>*So, I know our energy has to go somewhere.*</u>*"*

<u>*Darrell Thomas Crapo, April 2015*</u>

"That's right!" I blurted out loud; not of myself, but the Holy Spirit of God within me because I said it with such conviction even though I did not know why or how at the time. *"That energy is your spirit, your life, your very soul!"*

> **"And the LORD God formed man of dust of the ground, and breathed into his nostrils the breath of life; and man became a living soul."**

<u>*Genesis 2:7*</u> (KJV)

That conversation was on our last visit together which was just a week before his death. That visit occurred approximately three years before this intensive bible study with Jesus began. It was before I understood how Holy Spirit was working within me for the good according to His plan of salvation for my brother! All the glory to Father God! Hallelujah for The Trinity working marvelous wonders within us and through us! Amen!

> **"Have nothing to do with the fruitless deeds of darkness, but rather expose them."**

<u>*Ephesians 5:11*</u> (NIV)

And expose them I did! See how magnificent God's plans are? He made me speak of things I did not know of;

but Holy Spirit does because He is in communication with God! He is our direct access to Father God because of Jesus Christ and what He did at the Cross for us sinners! Our sister, Sharon Crapo Curry Chrysafis, was with brother during his last seconds. She said brother was awake when he looked up and reached up with his right hand! *Brother Darrell was left-handed!* He was not ambidextrous as our father was. No, he had been hard-core left handed all his life. That was all I needed to hear to believe that Darrell reached up and grabbed the right hand of Jesus Christ, accepting Him as his Savior! Amen!!!

> *"For I, the LORD your God, will hold your*
> *right hand, Saying to you,*
> *'Fear not, I will help you."*

Isaiah 41:13 (NKJV)

Reaching out with his right hand reminds me of the Scripture where Peter was walking on water toward Jesus, became distracted with the waves, and started to sink. Peter cried out for Jesus to save him...

> *"And immediately Jesus stretched out His*
> *hand and caught him, and said to him, 'O*
> *you of little faith, why did you doubt'?"*

Matthew 14:31 (NKJV)

I can just imagine hearing Jesus saying that to my brother, lovingly, of course. Brother had been seeking the truth and asking Sharon to read the Bible, God's plan of salvation... seek Him and you will find Him. That is how you draw near to GOD, by seeking Him.

"Come near to God and He will come near to you."

James 4:8 (NIV)

It is the mission of Christians, believers in Christ, to spread the gospel and plant seeds in the hearts and minds of the confused and the undecided. What if you were the very person that had a chance to be instrumental in planting seeds that lead someone to seek Christ? What if you were the one with an opportunity to get through to them? *What if you were the last one that could... and you said nothing?*

"...to turn them from darkness to light, and from the power of Satan to God, that they may receive forgiveness of sins, and inheritance among them which are sanctified by faith that is in Me."

Acts 26:18 (KJV)

If you are a nonbeliever, I will ask you now... " *What if you are wrong? And upon what are you basing your decision that affects your eternal soul?"* I implore you to seek the truth for yourself! Discover all the wonders of His Majestic Word, His promises found in the pages of The Holy Bible. But, most of all, discover His endless and unconditional agape (love) for you!

"And those who know Your name will put their trust in You;
For You, LORD, have not forsaken those who seek You."

Psalm 9:10 (NKJV)

What do you have to lose if you do not seek Jesus? I will tell you... your soul! What do you have to gain if you seek, find, and accept Jesus? I will tell you that too... your soul! You must believe and accept by faith that Jesus Christ is the Only Begotten Son of God, that He paid your sin debt and that He defeated death for you!

> *"For the law of the Spirit of Life in Christ Jesus hath made me free from the law of sin and death."*

Romans 8:2 (KJV)

I have faith that everything worked together bringing to fruition all the prayers and all the seeds that had been planted since Darrell's birth. All the glory to God! I have faith and belief that brother Darrell believed in God's plan of salvation that Sharon read to him over and over. I declare and believe that brother saw the Light of Jesus Christ, that he took hold of His right hand, and that he went with Jesus into paradise. That belief is in my heart by faith in God's Word as Truth!

> *"And Jesus said unto him, 'Verily I say unto thee, to day shalt thou be with Me in paradise.'"*

Luke 23:43 (KJV)

And I can almost hear Jesus saying to my brother, Darrell Thomas Crapo:

"Then He said to Thomas, 'Put your finger here; see my hands. Reach out your hand and put it into my side. Stop doubting and believe.'"

<u>John 20:27</u> (NIV)

"...and whoever lives by believing in Me will never die. Do you believe that?"

<u>John 11:26</u> (NIV)

Today is the fourth anniversary of the physical death of our brother, Darrell.
He is alive in heaven with Jesus and Momma.
Jesus... I believe!
Nanette Crapo 04/19/2019

-5-

ANOTHER PROPHETIC DREAM

"And it shall come to pass in the last days, saith GOD, I will pour out of My Spirit upon all flesh: and your sons and your daughters shall Prophesy, and your young men shall see visions, and your old men shall dream dreams."

<u>Acts 2:17</u> (KJV)

About three months after my brother Darrell passed from this world, my firstborn son, Anastasios II (Tasos), had a dream about someone he did not recognize. I was visiting him, and he told me about the following dream:

He said that I was at his house babysitting his son, Christian. Tasos and his wife, Amy, had just returned home when he saw a man *"with long wavy blonde hair down to his shoulders, standing at the curb in front of the house. He was holding a baby boy and standing beside a petite woman with brown hair. They were standing by a tricked out three wheeled motorcycle".* He continued to tell me that as he reached his front door, I opened it and he asked me who that man was. I exclaimed in my excitement, *"That's your uncle Darrell!"*

He described my brother as he looked in his early thirties. My son was just a very small child when my brother's hair was still blond and to his shoulders. Also, my brother and his wife had lost one of their twin sons midway through a pregnancy. My son did not know that Darrell had lost a baby boy. He also described Darrell's wife whom my son had not seen since he was about five years old. She was very petite and had passed away approximately three years before Darrell. My son did not know that either. Anyway, my son did not remember Darrell's wife, but he described both of them perfectly as they looked in their early thirties. And to top it off, my brother was definitely a motorcycle enthusiast! He had several over the years and took long bike rides with cousin, Clark Crapo, whenever he got the chance!

If I had been the one to dream that dream, it would not have meant anything significant to me because I would have recognized everyone in the dream. There was no other reason for my son to have that dream other than as an answer to my prayers. Praise be to GOD for my son's dream that I can envision my brother as a young man with long wavy blonde hair, reunited with his son and his wife and smiling... in heaven. The vision of my son's dream has replaced the vision I had of the last time I saw my brother.

Thank you Jesus! Thank you for reinforcing what I knew to be true in my heart!

> **"For God may speak in one way, or**
> **in another,**
> **Yet man does not perceive it.**
> **In a dream, in a vision of the night,**
> **When deep sleep falls upon men,**
> **While slumbering on their beds,**
> **Then He opens the ears of men,**
> **And seals their instruction."**
>
> ***Job 33:14-16*** (NKJV)

SECTION 2

FOURTH GENERATION SAVED

• • •

"I call heaven and earth as witnesses today against you,
that I have set before you life and death,
blessing and cursing;
therefore choose life,
that both you and your descendants
may live;"

<u>Deuteronomy 30:19</u> (NKJV)

❀ ❀ ❀

*"Believe on the LORD Jesus Christ, and
 you will be saved,
 you and your household."*
<u>*Acts 16:31*</u> (NKJV)

❀ ❀ ❀

CHAPTER 1

ANOINTING

o o o

"Enter into His gates with thanksgiving,
And into His courts with praise.
Be thankful to Him, and bless His name.
For the LORD is good;
His mercy is everlasting,
And His truth endures to all generations."

Psalms 100:4-5 (NKJV)

"And He took them up in His arms, put His
hands upon them, and blessed them."

Mark 10:16 (KJV)

I am now up to the fourth generation: from my Grandpa
Crapo to my mother to me and now to my sons. I am of the
belief that the devil can attack anyone, even our children. I
also have faith in the protective anointing power of christening my babies in the name of God the Father, God the
Son and God the Holy Spirit. I have faith that "dedicating"
them to God is giving them over to Him for His protection
until they can make their own decision of their own free
will. I also have faith that the bond between my children

and God cannot be broken and He has set the length of their time upon this earth. I have faith that it is so because it is written:

> *"...that you may love the LORD your God,*
> *that you may obey His voice,*
> *and that you may cling to Him,*
> *for He is your life and the length of*
> *your days;"*

Deuteronomy 30:20 (NKJV)

The following stories are concerning my two sons and the miracles that have saved them from harm time and time again. God is gracious and merciful to all that love Him, so introduce your children to Him as soon as possible. Think seriously about dedicating your infant(s) to God. Investigate the benefits of doing such so you can make an informed decision on the matter. As for me, I believe in my heart it was the very best thing I ever did for my two sons.

-1-
CHRISTENING And BAPTISM

> *"And the LORD spake unto Moses, saying,*
> *'Sanctify unto me all the firstborn, what-*
> *soever openeth the womb among the chil-*
> *dren of Israel, both of men and of beast:*
> *it is mine."*

Exodus 13:1-2 (KJV)

God has blessed me with two precious sons and a precious grandson. I was told that I may never have children, so they truly are miraculous blessings! Our first child came three years into our marriage and three years later came our second child. They are both cherished as the gifts from God that they are.

> **"Children are the crown of old men; and the glory of children are their fathers."**
>
> **Proverbs 17:6** (KJV)

My firstborn, Anastasios II (Tasos), was dedicated to Heavenly Father when he was eight months old. My second son, John Nicholas was also dedicated to God while still an infant. Both were Christened in the Greek Orthodox Church in Houston, Texas where we attended services with their father and grandparents.

I may have already said this before, but I will say it again; I am first and foremost a Christian as I follow Christ, my LORD and Savior. This journey is not about religion. It is all about seeking a closer one-on-one relationship with Him. And it is about passing the legacy of faith and love for Jesus, our Shepherd, to future generations; because He gave His life for us that we may have life eternal.

> **"I am the good Shepherd. The good shepherd gives His life for the sheep."**
>
> **John 10:11** (NKJV)

I can go into any of God's houses and worship Him. Key Word... "God's". I can and do worship Him all by myself sitting under a tree or in the middle of heavy traffic. I have faith that He is everywhere, and He hears and sees me wherever I

am. No one and nothing can take away what my Savior, Jesus Christ, lay down His life to give me! Amen!
  (From the journals of Nanette Crapo)

> *"Where can I go from Your Spirit?*
> *Or where can I flee from Your presence?"*
> *"If I take the wings of the morning,*
> *And dwell in the uttermost parts of the sea,*
> *Even there Your hand shall lead me,*
> *And Your right hand shall hold me."*

Psalm 139:7 & 9-10 (NKJV)

I dedicated my babies to God, their Maker, to form a bond with Him that I believe by faith no one and nothing can break. I can do nothing of myself in the way of protecting them or being with them every second of every day. It was and is my belief that they would be protected by the anointing of the christening until they became of age to choose of their own free will. I believed as an innocent child in what I could not see; and of course, I wanted the same for my children! In the event it was God's plan to take them early, I believed with all my heart that they would be received in heaven as children of God. That was my belief then and it remains my belief now. It is engrained deep within my heart.

> *"And He took them up in His arms, laid*
> *His hands on them, and blessed them."*

Mark 10:16 (NKJV)

There was another plus to having them christened. They were appointed godparents to care for them in the event something happened to us, the parents. The godparents of my firstborn son are his Greek grandparents. The godfather of my second son is his uncle, Sotiris Chrysafis, my sister's Greek husband. My mother and father, Mary and John Crapo, were honorary stand-ins. They could not be his godparents because they were not Greek nor were they of the Greek Orthodox faith. Regardless, my mother was thrilled to be "*baby John's*" appointed stand-in and vowed to spoil him. What can one say? Isn't that the way of every godparent and grandparent everywhere?

Anyway, one son accepted Jesus into his heart and was baptized at age twelve. But it was a battle with the devil himself for my other child. I praise God for His protection through the proverbial *prodigal son* years. I would like to mention that I truly believe the only reason the devil did not succeed is because he could not break the bond between my son and God Almighty. Also, there were many faith-filled prayers of a mother for her lost son. I prayed relentlessly and incessantly for three years, for the roaring lion was trying to devour my son through his peers at school. I give all the praise and all the glory to Father God for the miracle that touched my son's heart.

-2-
HOLY SPIRIT And A 9 mm SCREW
GOD Can Use Anything to Save a Soul

"*That the blessing of Abraham might come on the gentiles through Jesus Christ; that we might receive the promise of the Spirit through faith.*"

Galatians 3:14 (KJV)

**"Hear, O my son, and receive my sayings;
and the years of thy life shall be many,"**

Proverbs 4:10 (KJV)

There was a battle raging over the soul of one of my sons. I could see the change in him. He went from a happy, joyful boy to a sullen, angry teenager and I felt powerless to help him. Of course, I was powerless of myself; but through faith in the power of the name of Jesus in prayers, all things are possible. I had been praying for my son's salvation for three years, during which time he was heavily pursued by the devil through peer pressure at school.

I know he was saved from almost certain death on numerous occasions; a fact he did not know that I knew. I am just as certain he was saved from almost certain death on numerous occasions that I did not know about. God's undoubtedly had an army of angels surrounding him during those years, as always! It was time for him to make a choice between life or death for himself. God sent me the opportunity to give witness of the Holy Spirit within me to my son through a 9 mm screw. It was the miracle that turned him to Jesus, the Redeemer of our souls.

**"Thus, saith the LORD, thy Redeemer,
and He that formed thee from the womb,
I Am the LORD that maketh all things..."**

Isaiah 44:24 (KJV)

I had worked the night shift and by 9:00 am I was asleep. Suddenly, at around 9:30 am, I was awakened with the banging of kitchen cabinets. I heard loud groaning about a car part being needed. (For you auto mechanics that remember how the older cars were made, you probably already know which part was needed from the title of this story.) I got up, got dressed and went into the kitchen to see if I could help. My son explained to me that there was a missing screw, and his car would not start without that screw. He had driven it home and as long as the car was running it kept running; but once the engine was turned off, it would not restart without that screw.

The screw could have fallen off anywhere between his friend's house, which was about a mile away, and our driveway. I suggested a car parts place and he said they were just too expensive. I suggested a pick a part place and he said they would not sell just the screw. He would have to buy the whole (whatever it was) part to get the screw. Well, I expressed my condolences as I did not have the money to buy the three hundred dollar car part and he would have to wait at least a week. A week without his precious wheels!? Absurd! Unheard of! Sorry, nothing I could do at that time and I went back to bed. But God had a plan!

After tossing and turning for at least five minutes with a tugging at my heart to get up and help my son, (Holy Spirit at work here), I finally got out of bed and dressed a second time. I went outside where he was talking to a couple of his nefarious friends. He looked surprised and asked me what I was doing. I said, with an inner knowledge of certainty that surprised even me, *"I am going to find that screw for you."* I told him that I did not know how I knew but I had faith that Jesus was going to lead me to the screw to prove to him that He, Jesus, is real.

I started looking along the driveway, heading toward the street. He said he had already looked, and it was not there. He also told me I was wasting my time. So, again, I told him I would walk all the way to his friend's house if I had to because I had faith in God that I was going to find that screw! I felt very strongly in my gut (Holy Spirit again) that GOD wanted me to help my son look for that screw! And I felt just as strongly that it would be found!

I asked my son what the screw looked like, as I had not a clue. I mean, I know what a screw looks like; but they come in thousands of shapes and thousands of sizes! And there are lots of old screws lying around in the road! I needed a little help here! I needed a clue. What I got was a miracle! All the glory to Heavenly Father! In case you do not remember the definition of miracle that I used in an earlier chapter, I am referring to it again.

> **Miracle:** *"An event that exceeds the known laws of nature and science. Usually an act of God done through human agents."*

(NKJV DICTIONARY – CONCORDANCE p. 749)

In God's infinite wisdom and in keeping with the miraculous, the screw in question just happened to look like a 9 mm bullet with the threads of a screw. Well now! In the natural, what are the odds of that? But we were not dealing with the natural. God is supernatural and can supernaturally make bad things that happen to us work together for the good of those that believe.

> *"And we know that all things work together for good to those who love God, to those who are the called according to His purpose."*
>
> **Romans 8:28** (NKJV)

Now we were getting somewhere! I knew what a 9 millimeter bullet looked like as I had a 9 mm Taurus handgun. Armed with this new knowledge, I started down the street on the right-hand side of the road. I scanned from the center line over to the edge of the curb. My intention was to do the same on the other side of the street on my way back. In the natural one might have thought the screw should have been on the other side of the road as that is the side he was driving on to get home. But that did not matter to me either. I was being guided and I was giving this search all of my attention. Besides, it was not of my efforts; it was the prompting of Holy Spirit as to which side of the road I was to start my search... unseen forces at work!

About 90 yards from our driveway, still on the right-hand side of the road, I saw it! It was nestled against the curb at the foot of a driveway. Let me tell you, it really did look like a 9 mm bullet! Thank you, Jesus! I did not detect the threads until I picked it up, but I already knew it was the missing screw! I just knew without the glimmer of a doubt... I just knew. It was a miracle from God in answer to the prayers of a mother for her prodigal son's return. Thank You Abba Father God! Thank You Jesus!

> *"For as many as are led by the Spirit of God, these are sons of God."*
>
> **_Romans 8:14_** (NKJV)

As I turned, I yelled, "*I found it!*" He was still standing at the foot of our driveway watching my every move and no doubt laughing at me. I held my prize high up in the air! He just stood there in bewilderment and asked, "*What?*" By this time, I was walking back as briskly as I could because I was excited to give it to him!

I yelled again that I had *"found it"*. Again, he just stood there, looking at me. Apparently, he really could not hear me yet, as he again asked, *"What?"* I was covering ground as fast as I could without running, although I wanted to run. I was watching him as I said a third time, *"I found it!"* He stared a few seconds longer in disbelief, then said one of his favorite phrases, *"No way!"* I had the pleasure of saying, *"Yes way!"* Another short pause by him as it all sunk in.

All of a sudden he started running toward me! He did not even look at the screw in my hand when he reached me! Do you know why? Because the instant Jesus touched his heart with faith... he knew that I had the screw and that God had led me straight to it! He just grabbed me around my neck and said, "Momma! I believe!" There we were, in the middle of the street, holding on to each other and crying tears of relief, tears of joy and a momma's tears of thanksgiving to God for answering her prayers! Amen!

(Taken from the journals of Nanette Crapo)

This story still brings tears of joy to my eyes! All the glory to Father God for touching my son's heart with the love of Jesus and saving his soul. I can rest in peace that both my children have the promise of eternal life through faith in Jesus Christ. We are truly blessed.

> **"For this my son was dead, and is alive again, he was lost, and is found. And they began to be merry."**
>
> ***Luke 15:24*** (KJV)

"Likewise, I say to you, there is joy in the presence of the angels of God over one sinner who repents."

Luke 15:10 (NKJV)

CHAPTER 2

ANGELS AND MIRACLES

•••

"But the Lord is faithful, who will establish you and guard you from the evil one."

2 Timothy 3:3 (NKJV)

This chapter is full of individual stories about some of the many miracles that have saved both of my children from certain and / or almost certain death, possibly with the intervention of His angels. I say that to differentiate between Holy Spirit leading me to a 9 mm screw vs other forms of divine interventions. I was surprised to learn that my children remember many of these incidents, especially those that occurred when they were very young. But, then again, I have vivid memories of things that occurred when I was a baby… so why not? There have been many more miracles that have saved their lives, and I can only surmise that God has plans for them.

I would like to mention that I sometimes refer to the Holy Spirit of God as "the Holy Spirit of God" and sometimes as "Holy Spirit". When I speak of Him as the third person of the Godhead, the Trinity, I say, "God the Holy Spirit" or "the Holy Spirit of God". Otherwise, He is "Holy

Spirit" as that is His name. It is the same in my mind as referring to Jesus as "God the Son" or the Son of God". I would not call Jesus, "the Jesus" as that is not His name. This is my personal preference because it makes my relationship with Jesus and Holy Spirit that much more intimate to me.

-1-
Angels And The Toy Car

> *"But the mercy of the LORD is from ever-lasting to everlasting upon them that fear him, and his righteousness unto children's children;"*

Psalm 103:17 (KJV)

This first story involves both my children. The three of us were leaving a department store where both had gotten new toy cars. Tasos, my firstborn son, had his car clutched in his hand tightly as his little brother, John, was trying to take it away from him. They were both in the front seat without seatbelts or car seats. This was before laws to place children in the back seat in car seats and before laws requiring seat-belts were put into place. In fact, my car did not even have seatbelts.

Let me back up a bit and explain the scenario. Tasos had been trying to take John's car away. John was crying and Tasos was fighting with him. I finally decided to take mat-ters into my own hands as my nerves were about to crack with all the commotion. So, I confiscated John's car, rolled down my window, and pretended to throw it away. That was a mistake! Both boys sat in stunned silence for a few seconds; then they started all over again! This time, John was trying to take Tasos's car away from him. Just as I was making a left-hand turn on the inside of a double lane turn, Tasos decided he would throw his car away as well!

However, instead of rolling his window down, he opened the car door and fell out on his head, right in the middle of the double turning lanes! All I heard was *swoosh!* I looked around just in time to see his little feet disappear! I screamed and I could not stop the car fast enough. When the car finally stopped, it was in the middle of oncoming traffic as I had been turning in front of them at the light.

As I jumped out, I noticed my car rolling forward! I had left it in gear with the motor running with my baby sitting on the armrest! (Those old cars had high armrests that folded up or down, depending on if you wanted to use them or not. It made the perfect seat for my two-year-old.) I jumped back into the car, stopped the motor, jumped out again, and ran as fast as I could to my child lying motionless in the middle of that busy intersection; again, leaving my baby in the car... alone! *I was insane with fear and clearly not thinking straight!*

By the time I finally reached Tasos, he was just waking up, still clutching his toy car in his precious little hand. There were two strangers kneeling over him. The man was a doctor, and his wife was a nurse. They were on their way to work at a hospital that was literally blocks away. Tasos was still a baby himself, age five, and was scared, as you can imagine! The couple had called for an ambulance because Tasos had been unconscious when they had reached him. The ambulance arrived within a few minutes, and Tasos was calm until they started to put him inside. That's when he lost it. I could see the fear and panic in his eyes. He had watched enough television to know what an ambulance was, and I think he thought he would never see me again.

Well, I hopped right in the back of that ambulance and rode with my hysterical child. No, I did not forget about John. The doctor's wife drove my car to the hospital with John still perched upon the middle armrest, calmly watching everything go down. John was always the one to quietly observe while in deep thought; even at such an early age. He did not cry when I left him, and he did not cry when the stranger got into the car beside him and drove away without his momma and his brother.

In today's time I would be too suspicious and fearful to allow a stranger to take charge of one of my children. I would have insisted that he go in the ambulance with me. (The ambulance attendants told me that I was not allow to bring John with me.) I had to choose, and of course, I chose to go with the frightened, injured child. I thank God for His angels and His miracles!

God is always with us. His Holy Spirit dwells within us because of the sacrifice Jesus made for us at the Cross. And, because we believe in Jesus Christ as God's only Begotten Son that was sent to die in our place to pay our monumental sin debt, we receive His promise of everlasting life. Regardless, God is everywhere all the time! He is watching believers and nonbelievers alike! He does not miss a thing! I am a believer in His Precious Son, Jesus Christ, Yeshua, The Messiah, and I know in my heart that He immediately sent an army of His angels to our rescue; because it is written:

> **"For He shall give His angels charge over thee..."**
>
> **Psalm 91:11** *(KJV)*

You will never convince me that angels were not involved! They prevented Tasos from falling under my own back tire! The way I was turning, there was no way in the natural that he landed where he did without jumping out of the car; which, he did not do. He simply fell out from the momentum of the turn... headfirst! He could have had a severe head injury and a severe road rash. He had neither. He did suffer a mild concussion; but other than that, there was not a mark on him. You cannot tell me that God's mighty hand of protection was not upon him, preventing him from getting up and running through the cars after me! And I believe God had more angels standing guard around my motionless son as the cars in both turning lanes missed running over him. That in itself was a miracle!

Then there were the angels that He sent to watch over John. They kept him from getting out of the car and running after mommy; something I did not even consider he might do. I was in panic mode! As attached as he was to me, only the angels kept him in that car! I had even left my car door open and the keys in the ignition! God is awesome and full of miracles. No one can tell me He is not real! It was by His grace and mercy that He sent angels and Good Samaritans to protect both of my children at the same time while I was incapacitated with anxiety and fear for my child.

Thank You, Abba, Father GOD! Thank You, Jesus, (Yeshua), our Savior! Thank You Holy Spirit!

-2-
SUPERMAN
And The
SUPERHERO
At The PARTHENON

"They shall bear thee up in their hands,
least thou dash thy foot against a stone."

Psalm 91:12 (KJV)

Our vacation to Athens, Greece does not have pleasant memories for me. I wanted to go sightseeing on this once in a lifetime trip, but that was only on the itinerary twice during the three weeks there. We were mainly there to visit with my husband's relatives, friends and the friends of his mother. I was just along for the ride.

One such sightseeing excursion was to the Parthenon. I was pregnant with John and Tasos was about two-and-one-half years old. The movie Superman was out, and we had seen it two or three times. Tasos owned a little red cape as most children his age at the time did. One of my husband's childhood friends, Dimitris Chrysafis, was our guide that day. He became more than just our guide. He turned just in time to see Tasos standing on the low wall of the ruins of the Parthenon, arms outstretched in true Superman launch mode!

In the instant Tasos said, "*up, up and away*!" and jumped off the wall, Dimitris grabbed him! Let me tell you… Dimitris grabbed Tasos after he had already jumped! It was as if Tasos was outside of time itself and for a split second was suspended in mid-air! I had heard of such things happening. Years later, my youngest son, John, experienced this phenomenon while on vacation. (*Angels On Vacation*) I myself have experienced being *outside of time* twice *(Peace in Chaos* and one other time not mentioned in this book). No one will ever convince me that it is not possible!

> **"Jesus said, 'What is impossible with man is possible with God.'"**
>
> **_Luke 18:27_** (NIV)

Just because it is beyond our intellectual capacity to understand miracles does not make them fables or coincidences. Anyway, that split second is all it took for Dimitris to grab our son, literally by the seat of his pants, and save him from the sheer drop-off to the jagged rocks below! It was not a coincidence that Dimitris was with us that day. He turned out to be more than our guide; he was our superhero!

All the praise and glory belongs to Father God for His impeccable timing to have the right person with us that day. I thank you, Dimitris, for answering God's calling to be our tour guide that day; placing you in the right place at the right time to save our son as he took flight! I thank Abba, Father God, for His mighty breath and His angels that halted the airborne flight of Tasos for the split second it took for Dimitris to grab him, saving him from certain death! And I will repeat myself; there is no such thing as coincidence or luck! No one on this planet has luck that can match the grace and mercy of the miracles of God Almighty... no one!

Nanette Crapo May 25, 2019

"It is of the LORD'S mercies that we are not consumed, because His compassions fail not."

Lamentation 3:22 (KJV)

-3-
"UP, UP AND AWAY!"
Superman Flies Again!

*"Bless the LORD, ye His angels, that excel
in strength, that do His commandments,
hearkening unto the voice of His word."*

Psalm 103:20 (KJV)

Same hero's cry, different child. John, now almost five years old, uttered those same famous words as he jumped off the second story balcony of an apartment building! The devil would have had him fall upon the decorative spears of the wrought iron fence just a few feet away from the building; but by the grace of God's mercy through the Blood of Jesus Christ, John was caught up in the arms of angels, and I will not be convinced otherwise! Although I could not see them, it was impossible in the natural for John to land where he did; so I know what I know!

The landing was a miracle in itself. John was taken (*dare I say flew*?) beyond the fence to a soft mushy patch of ground and was completely unharmed. There was no way in the natural that a small child could have jumped that far without the supernatural intervention of God! I never will cease to give God all the glory for all the miracles that have saved my children, time and time again! *Thank You, Father God, in the name of Jesus… again*!

Faith in and love for the Sacrificial Lamb of God has sustained us through the good and the bad for five generations. Without belief in the redeeming power of His precious Blood, everything else would be pointless. Jesus demonstrated His tremendous, immeasurable agape kind of love for us when He paid our sin debt by sacrificing His life for ours. We belong to Jesus. No one and nothing can shorten the length of days that God has appointed to us by snatching us out of His hands or the hands of Jesus.

> *"And I give them eternal life, and they shall never perish, neither shall anyone snatch them out of my hand. My Father, who has given them to Me, is greater than all; and no one is able to snatch them out of My father's hand."*

> **John 10:28-29** (NKJV)

I give my thanks and my heart to Jesus for all He suffered for us to make our Salvation possible!

For anyone that has not accepted Jesus Christ as their LORD and Savior, let me encourage you to do so without delay, because time is running out. You may not have tomorrow to decide. In fact, you may not have one more minute. Jesus is returning soon and without warning! God alone knows when Jesus Christ will return, and when He does it will be within the twinkling of the eye. That is not enough time to prepare to be saved. The time to accept Jesus as your LORD and Savior is now.

> *"But of that day and hour no one knows, not even the angels of heaven, but My Father only."*

> **Matthew 24:36** *(NKJV)*

-4-
ANGELS ON VACATION

Do not let the subtitle mislead you. Angels do not get vacations; especially, when watching over children. They are always on high alert! If it were not so, none of us would live very long. Without God's protection, none of us would survive the devil's evil schemes and none of us would have a testimony to share!

No, angels do not get vacations, but they were with us on ours and for that I praise God! This story occurred while we were on vacation to California. We stopped at Hoover Dam to stretch our legs and do a little sight-seeing. There is (or was) a wall approximately five feet tall with a very thick glass, or plexiglass, on top of it. However, a small area to the left and to the right had only the wall itself. There was not an extension of glass or plexiglass of any kind! Do not ask me why, but that is where I was standing when my youngest son, John, came flying past me like a bolt of lightning! I could envision him sailing right over that wall and all the way to the bottom! I could also envision myself jumping after him, catching him, and holding him all the way to our deaths. I could not imagine living without even one of my children! Of course, catching him would have been impossible in the natural; but, in my terror-stricken visions I thought it would have been possible if it had come to that. It is difficult even now, some thirty years later, to recall what happened without cringing within my heart of what could have been without God's intervention.

John was just shy of five feet tall and could not see over the wall to the abyss beyond! He had no idea how far down the drop off was. He has since told me he took the running jump to get up on the wall to spit on the other side! He also told me that when he saw how far down it was he forgot about spitting! I am here to give testimony that I watched as my son went past me in slow motion, yet so fast that I did not have time to react! It is hard to explain... surreal. Then suddenly, a forceful gust of wind came at us head-on. That wind was so strong that it stopped him and caused him to land on his stomach on top of a two foot wide ledge! It was supernaturally forceful and seemed to me to suspend John in the air! It's sheer force nearly knocked me backward! My heart skipped several beats as it dropped into the pit of my stomach!

> **"So the men marveled, saying, 'Who can this be, that even the winds and the sea obey Him'?"**
>
> **_Matthew 8:27_** (NKJV)

Reminiscing causes me anxiety. I go to God in prayer for the peace of Jesus to return to me after such visits into the past. I thank Heavenly Father and Jesus daily for His hedge of protection that surrounds my children, my grandchild, me, and all my extended family! I have no explanation other than God sent His angels to halt my son's flight, grabbed him and placed him upon that wall; and I thank God that His angels do not get vacations!

> **"I have spoken to you of earthly things and you do not believe; how then will you believe if I speak of heavenly things?"**
>
> **_John 3:12_** (NIV)

CHAPTER 3

BABY POWDER...
The Devil Can
Weaponize Anything

• • •

"No weapon formed against you shall prosper,"

<u>*Isaiah 54:17*</u> (NKJV)

My youngest son, John, was barely ten months old when he was attacked with baby powder! He was at a day care that used baby powder a little too freely. They fluffed and puffed a liberal amount upon him with each diaper change. When he went to bed, he was just fine; but, when I woke him up to get him ready for the nursery so I could go to work, he was listless! He was also red hot and candy apple red! I did not even have a thermometer in the house! Here I was, a nurse, and I didn't know what to do when it was my own in trouble! So much for calm in chaos when baby bear is in distress! I remember calling in to cancel work as I was sponging him off with tepid water. That made him start crying! I imagine it felt like ice water on his burning skin. I did not waste much time on that endeavor because I was fearful of a pending seizure!

As quickly as I could grab John, my keys and my purse, we were off to the emergency room. It was only about a year later that my firstborn son was taken to that same ER after falling out of our car head-first! By the time we got there he was an ominous dark purplish red and having trouble breathing. They took him right away and saved him with medicated breathing treatments to open his airway and medications for his fever. They told me he had an asthma attack. I told them that he had never even had the sniffles before; but, they said to expect him to be asthmatic the rest of his life with more attacks! God had other plans for my son!

> *"But He was wounded for our transgressions, He was bruised for our iniquities: the chastisement of our peace was upon Him; and with His stripes we are healed."*
>
> *Isaiah 53:5* (KJV)

I changed nurseries and John never had another "asthma attack" as a child. So, I cannot tell you exactly what the miracles were. Did God miraculously cure him from his asthma or from the one-time effects of inhaled baby powder? Either way it was a miracle! It was a miracle I got to him in time to get him to the hospital! It was a miracle he did not stop breathing or have lasting neurological effects from lack of oxygen! John had been christened and I am convinced he was and is covered by the Blood of Jesus Christ; the Blood of the Lamb of God!

Thank You, Jesus, Yeshua, for suffering the stripes in your flesh for our healing! Thank You, Father God, for your angels that are always watching, waiting and protecting my children and my grandchild!

Nanette Crapo April 2019

"You intended to harm me, but God intended it for good to accomplish what is now being done, the saving of many lives."

Genesis 50:20 (NIV)

CHAPTER 4

HOLY SPIRIT VS DEVIL'S SCHEMES GOOD VS EVIL

● ● ●

*"And His mercy is on them that fear Him
from generation to generation."*

Luke 1:50 (KJV)

In the following stories, God utilized objects to thwart the attacks of the devil and his evil schemes.

*"He will not allow your foot to be moved;
He who keeps you will not slumber.
Behold, He who keeps Israel
Shall neither slumber nor sleep."*

Psalm 121:3-4 (NKJV)

-1-
HOLY SPIRIT VS A 22 SLUG

"You shall not be afraid of the terror by night, Nor of the arrow that flies by day,"

<u>*Psalm 91:5*</u> (NKJV)

Once upon a time, long ago, we lived in an unsafe neighborhood for about seven years. My youngest son, John, was in martial arts and had advanced through several belts. Each level of achievement advanced him to another color of belt for his uniform. By the time of this next chain of miracles, he had accumulated at least five or six different colored belts from white to red. I do not remember exactly how many belts he had nor all the colors; but the green one became my favorite.

It all started when our home was burglarized. The thieves had come in through John's bedroom window which prompted me (by Holy Spirit which guides me even when I am not aware of it) to move John's bed from in front of the window. I replaced it with his chest of drawers because it was much heavier and blocked the window from intruders. That move in itself was a miracle. *Thank You Jesus!* If John's bed had still been in front of that window, he would have been shot in the head while he slept!

For some unknown reason(s) we were the victims of a drive by spraying of bullets! Shortly after midnight, we were awakened with the sound of rapid gunfire! Bullets sprayed the front and the back of our home simultaneously. The entire family met in the living room after the barrage of gunfire, all frightened and in dazed disbelief! That's the kind of stuff one only sees on the news... isn't it? There were no houses behind us, only another street. The bricks did not let any of the bullets penetrate into the house. However, the windows across the back of the house and in John's room at the front of the house afforded no protection at all! There were bullets lodged in the living room wall. John's bedroom and the new position of his bed was on the other side of that wall. No bullets penetrated the paneling or the sheetrock, but were lost somewhere in between!

When morning came, we inspected the outside of the house and found damaged bricks from numerous bullets. It was only from the outside that I could see the bullet hole in John's bedroom window! I ran inside and looked all around his room. I could not find any exit holes on his dresser, so I looked inside of the drawers. There nestled inside the thick green martial arts belt was a 22 slug! The belt was rolled up, as they all were, so the slug only made it past the first layer; getting trapped in the second layer. That belt was level with where my son's head would have been just a day or two before! If I had not been prompted to move his bed there would have been nothing to stop that bullet from reaching John as he slept! God even protects us while we are asleep!

There were multiple miracles at work here:

- The robbery itself was turned to the good to save John's life;
- Holy Spirit prompted me to move John's bed because of the robbery;
- The belts were in the right drawer at the right appointed time; and
- There were no injuries during the onslaught of 22 slugs!

God does not sleep and neither do His angels! All the glory to Father God!

"My help comes from the LORD,
Who made heaven and earth.
He will not allow your foot to be moved;
He who keeps you will not slumber."

Psalm 121:2-3 (NKJV)

-2-
HOLY SPIRIT VS THE GAS LEAK

"Because you have made the LORD, who
is my refuge,
Even the most High, your dwelling place,
No evil shall befall you,
Nor shall any plague come near your
dwelling;"

Psalm 91:9-10 (NKJV)

This is the last of the chapter about miracles; but believe me, it is by far not the last of the miracles. I have enough to fill another book. It was difficult to choose which miraculous stories to use. This one involved both my children and myself when we were all much younger and on our own in a rented house. We had been there several weeks when the boys got a bunny for Easter. After only a few days, the poor little bunny was found dead in the garage! I had no idea at the time what had happened to it. Then a day or so later the following miracles occurred. I declare them to be supernatural miracles as there simply is no other explanation in the natural. I do not believe in "luck". God was, is and always will be in complete control of everything!

"My help comes from the LORD, the Maker of heaven and earth."

Psalm 121:2 (NIV)

My two sons were fast asleep, and I was in bed. This was back in the days when I first started smoking. I was out of cigarettes and could not go to the store as my children were already asleep. I decided to tough it out till morning and buy some on the way to work because I was so very sleepy. Just when I closed my eyes... the phone rang.

It was a house phone. In this day and age they are called land lines. Cell phones were not available. (I told you, we were all much younger then.) I did not have any real friends of my own, and my phone never rang unless it was work or my sister. To receive an unexpected call from someone that was just checking up on how I was doing on that particular night was a miracle in itself; because it was not my work, and it was not my sister. It was someone that felt led to give me a call and check on how I was doing. (Really!) This person asked if I had been drinking because they said my speech was slurred. I insisted that I had not, and knowing me they believed me! I told them I had a headache which was rare for me and I was very sleepy. I was told to open all the windows. After discovering every window was stuck tight with new paint, I was told to get my boys and get out of the house, "*immediately*!" All I wanted to do was go to sleep, but I did as I was told because of the urgency in the voice on the phone. I called my brother Max on my way out the door. Max called my sister, Sharon, and my brother-in-law Sotiris. They all arrived at the same time, and we waited outside together until the gas company came and shut off the gas. Indeed, we had a gas leak!

So, the following are what I can only explain as miracles from God that occurred through circumstances and the intervention of other people. God can use anything and anyone to intervene on our behalf.

- If I had not been out of cigarettes... I could have blown us all up!
- If my phone had not rang... I wouldn't be here to give this testimony!
- If I had already been asleep... we would not have awakened the next morning! I take that back; we would have awakened... in heaven. Amen!

Thank You Father God for all You have done, all You do and all You will do for my children, my family, myself and the world, even though we do not deserve it! Where would we be without Your mercy, Your grace and Your great love? Where would we be without Your Precious Son, Jesus Christ, our Savior? I tremble to think about that! And to think how much I complained about things that seem so irrelevant now! Thank You Jesus for loving us so much that You took our place on the Cross and freed us from death, hell and the grave. Only You are Worthy, Jesus, to be the Lamb of God. There is no other!
Nanette Crapo, May 2019

> **"For I will pour water upon him that is thirsty, and floods upon the dry ground: I will pour my spirit upon thy seed and my blessing upon thine offspring: ..."**

Isaiah 44:3 (KJV)

CHAPTER 5

MORE VISIONS
and DREAMS

o o o

> *"And it shall come to pass afterward,*
> *that I will pour out my Spirit upon all*
> *flesh; and your sons and your daugh-*
> *ters shall prophesy, your old men shall*
> *dream dreams, your young men shall see*
> *visions: ..."*

Joel 2:28 (KJV)

My youngest son, John, has also had prophetic dreams as well as visions. When he was approximately four years of age, he had a vision of a spirit one evening when I was away at work. He saw the spirit (perhaps an angel) of "*a woman dressed all in white*" like my nursing uniform, He said he thought it was me until she turned and walked through his bedroom wall! He remembers he was feeling very sad because of something his father said or did, he could not remember the details. He does remember that he was alone in his room and he was crying.

When he saw the vision, spirit, apparition or whatever it was, he spoke to it because he thought it was me, his mother, in my nursing uniform. This was before nurses were allowed to wear the colored two piece scrubs that they wear today. Nurses were still wearing white dresses with white shoes and white stockings or white pant suits from the uniform store, and a white nursing cap. John said that when he spoke the woman turned and walked through the wall. He said he never saw her again.

I remember telling him it was probably an angel sent to comfort him. But instead of comforting him, he was frightened; so I highly doubt my first impression. He remembers it to this day, and it happened over thirty years ago. He said it still gives him chills to think about that incident. He has admitted to having other visions and many dreams. It definitely runs in the family! I have encouraged him to write them down.

I will leave the rest of my two son's prophetic visions and dreams for them to tell one day; if they so desire and if God calls them to do so. Remember my firstborn son, Tasos? He had the prophetic dream that was pertinent to my testimony about my brother Darrell's salvation. Both could fill a book of their own with miracles, visions, dreams and the occasional discerning of (good and evil) spirits. They both have powerful testimonies to give as to the reality of the gospel of Jesus Christ; His Majesty, His power, His protection and His love in their lives.

God speaks to all of us through many forms of communication. Some of my dreams have insightful revelations from God. I have recognized some of them as such right away and the meaning of some were revealed to me weeks or months later. Some are very profound and revealing i.e. the one about generational curses and asps. (I will have to save that for another book, perhaps.) Others have been answers to prayers, warnings, directions, etc. And I admit that some do not seem to mean anything at all... right now. But look how long it took for me to understand the prophesy of the dream I had as a child about my brother in the water with the sharks!

The ones that do not seem to mean anything now, I will reread because some of them just may jump at me later with a profound revelation! Only God knows. No telling how many I have had that I do not remember because I did not write them down. Sad, for they are lost forever. I pay closer attention now, and keep a pen and notepad at my bedside, because I do not want to miss a single Word from Heavenly Father!

> *"In a dream, in a vision of the night,*
> *When deep sleep falls upon men,*
> *While slumbering on their beds,*
> *Then He opens the ears of men,*
> *And seals their instruction."*
>
> ***Job 33:15-16*** (NKJV)

SECTION 3

FIFTH GENERATION BLESSED

• • •

"*For you know that it was not with perishable things such as silver or gold that you were redeemed from the empty way of life handed down from your ancestors, but with the precious blood of Christ, a lamb without blemish or defect.*"

1 Peter 1:18-19 (NIV)

◦ ◦ ◦

"Tell your children about it,
Let your children tell their children,
And their children another generation."

<u>Joel 1:3</u> (NKJV)

◦ ◦ ◦

CHAPTER 1

CONSECRATION OF
THE FIRSTBORN

• • •

*"In whom we have redemption through
His blood, even the forgiveness of sins:
Who is the image of the invisible God, the
firstborn of every creature:"*

<u>*Colossians 1: 14-15*</u> (KJV)

*"and all the firstborn of man among thy
children shall thou redeem."*

<u>*Exodus 13:13*</u> (KJV)

In The Old Testament of <u>The Holy Bible,</u> in the Book
of Exodus, it is written that the only way to redeem the
firstborn child was with the sacrificial blood of a firstborn
male animal. That is why the firstborn males of all the ani-
mals were God's as well; their blood was sacrificed to redeem
"the firstborn of man among thy children..." (Exodus 13:13).
That was before Jesus. Jesus is the firstborn of God, *"the firstborn of every creature..."* (Colossians 1:15) that opened the

womb, "*born of a woman*" (Galatians 4:4). Jesus is the sacrificial Lamb of God, "*in whom we have redemption through His blood...*" (Colossians 1:14). When we accept Jesus as our Savior, we are born again; redeemed by His Blood, the blood of God's Firstborn. Maybe you are thinking that only applies to the children of Israel, the Jewish people? But it is written, we gentiles (non-Jews) have been adopted as the children of God through Jesus Christ, Yeshua our Messiah. His blood, shed at Calvary, made adoption possible for those that believe in Him as the Son of God, and accept Him as their LORD and Savior.

> "*...God sent His Son, born of a woman, born under the law, to redeem those under the law, that we might receive adoption to sonship.*"

Galatians 4:4-5 (NIV)

You may be asking yourself, "*Wasn't Adam God's firstborn?*". Scripture clearly states that Adam was:

> "*...formed of the dust of the ground...*"

Genesis 2:7 (NKJV)

So, the answer is, "*No, Adam was not God's firstborn.*" Adam was not born of a woman and neither was Eve. Adam was, however, given dominion over all the earth, but lost that dominion to Satan. It is important to know why he lost dominion over all of God's creation because most of us are guilty of the same sin... disobedience to God. I am sure a lot of you readers know the story about the Garden of Eden. Satan used the serpent to tempt Eve by putting doubt in her mind that God did not really mean what He said when He told them if they ate of the tree of knowledge of good and evil, they would die.

God *cannot lie:*

> *"I have sworn by myself, the word is gone out of my mouth in righteousness, and shall not return..."*
>
> *Isaiah 45:23* (KJV)
>
> *"... which God, who cannot lie, promised before time began..."*
>
> *Titus 1:2* NKJV)

Eve did eat the forbidden fruit and in turn she tempted Adam and he also ate it. They opened the door for sin and death upon mankind because of their disobedience to God.

> *"For as by one man's disobedience many were made sinners, so also by one Man's obedience many will be made righteous."*
>
> *Romans 5:19* (NKJV)

Here are some key points to remember:

- God gave dominion over the earth to Adam (mankind). (Genesis 1:26)
- God commanded they were not to eat of the fruit of the tree of knowledge of good and evil or they would die. (Genesis 1:16-17)

- Adam and Eve sinned and became cursed when they ate the forbidden fruit. (Genesis 3:15-19)
- Sin was released upon mankind because of disobedience to God. (Romans 5:19)
- Death was released upon mankind because of disobedience. (Genesis 3:17-19)
- Adam lost dominion through sin and death. (Romans 5:7)
- Jesus freed us of sin, reclaiming dominion over death. (Roman 6:7-9); (Ephesians 1:20-21)

"For he who has died has been freed from sin. Now if we died with Christ, we believe that we shall also live with Him, knowing that Christ, having been raised from the dead, dies no more. Death no longer has dominion over Him."

<u>Romans 6:7-9</u> (NKJV)

Jesus took all of our sins upon Himself as the only worthy Sacrificial Lamb of God… without blemish and without sin. When Jesus was nailed to the Cross in our place, He satisfied the payment under the law for our sin debt which was and is death. He paid it in full with His very own Life's Blood. He did it for the whole world which includes you. Yes, Jesus suffered and died in your place because He loves you and He wants to spare you from eternal darkness. When Jesus paid our sin debt, He reclaimed dominion over death, hell and the grave. By His grace, Jesus gives us life. That is the mystery of Jesus Christ, our Savior.

Nanette Crapo April 21, 2019

"For if by the one man's offense death reigned through the one, much more those who receive abundance of grace and of the gift of righteousness will reign in life through the One, Jesus Christ."

Romans 5:17 (NKJV)

As I have previously mentioned, I believe there is protection for our children when we have them christened, or dedicated and set apart for God while they are yet infants. It is something that as parents we are responsible for; protecting our young. Who better than we to protect them?... the Lamb of God, that's who. Since we by ourselves are helpless against the devil and his evil scheme's, we need God's protection for our young ones! It was something that God placed into my heart to do. I did not know the above scriptures about sanctifying and consecrating one's firstborn as I was unfamiliar with the knowledge that one can find in The Holy Bible. It was one of those times that I knew I should do it because... well, I just knew without knowing how I knew... I just knew. Now I realize Holy Spirit was guiding me in God's ways on the subject for the benefit of my children. And for all those years I thought it was my idea.

If I had known the knowledge of God's Word, if I had read it, I would have known how I knew; and I would have listened to that inner voice of Holy Spirit more closely and wisely. The old saying about hindsight being 20/20 is so very true. The key is to get that 20/20 vision in advance through God's Word. It is not too late for us to start with our future, our children, and all the generations to come. If not us, then who?

"In all their affliction He was afflicted,

And the Angel of His Presence saved them;
In His love and in His pity
He redeemed them;
And He bore them and carried them
All the days of old."

Isaiah 63:9 (NKJV)

CHAPTER 2

A BOY
NAMED CHRISTIAN

❦❦❦

*"Just because my name is Christian doesn't
mean I follow Christ... (slight thoughtful
pause)... but I do."*

**Christian Alexander Karamitsos, Age 7
September 2019**

In the summer and early fall of 2019, I had the privi-
lege of spending quality time with my only grandchild,
Christian. One day while in the formal living room, which
had French doors allowing for privacy, I was sitting alone
watching my favorite Christian network when he came
in and quietly sat down beside me. He called that room
"Grandma's Church" because I always had the television on
a Christian channel. He was curious about hearing his name
mentioned so much. This opened the discussion about what
makes a person a *"Christian"*. He is 7 years old and seeking:

> **"Ask, and it will be given to you; seek,
> and you will find; knock, and it will be
> opened to you."**

Matthew 7:7 (NKJV)

I explained that a Christian believes in Jesus Christ as the Son of God. I told him the word *Christian* describes people that follow Christ.

> **"So it was that for a whole year they assem-
> bled with the church and taught a great
> many people. And the disciples were first
> called Christians in Antioch."**

Acts 11:26 (NKJV)

After deep thought for several moments he spoke these words:

> **"Just because my name is Christian doesn't
> mean I follow Christ...** (slight thoughtful
> pause)... **but I do."**

**Christian Alexander Karamitsos,
Age 7, September 2019**

I told Christian it made me very happy to hear him say that he follows Jesus Christ. I told him that he has special gifts from God such as love and compassion for others. I have witnessed him taking up for the weak when he sees them being bullied. I told him that makes him a superhero and it makes Jesus happy. He has other gifts as well such as kindness and joy. He likes helping his mother doing crafts and helping his father cook on the grill. He makes friends easily and shares his toys. I could go on and on about recognizing the *fruit of the Spirit* (Galatians 5:22-23) within him. The important thing is, he loves Jesus, and that relationship needs to be nourished.

> ***"Consecrate to Me all the firstborn, whatever opens the womb among the children of Israel, both of men and beast; it is Mine."***

Exodus 13: 1-2 (NKJV)

I do not remember if I mentioned in an earlier chapter or not, but Christian is the third generation of firstborn males. I explained to him that God had special plans for his future and one day those plans would be told to him by God. I expected more questions about this, but instead, Christian said with such sincerity, *"I know things sometimes that I don't know how I know... I just know."* Wow! That blew granny away! He is only 7 years old and already he hears his Shepperd's voice though he does not even understand it for what it is... yet!

On another day, Christian came in quietly and sat down beside me while I was in my *"Church"*. Again, he showed me he was seeking; that is always a good thing. He said sometimes he hears noises at night, and they scare him. I told him Jesus is always with him and will protect him from scary things. He listened intently as I explained to him if he felt afraid, he could call out the name of *"Jesus"* and the scary noises had to leave him alone. I stressed the importance of saying *"leave me alone in the name of Jesus"*, because the power comes from His Holy name... *"Jesus"*.

He liked what he heard. He said, *"That's good to know."* He is wise beyond his years, that's for sure. I do not boast just because he is my grandson. His intelligence leaves me in awe. I miss him and can hardly wait till next summer. I hope to spend more quality time with him. There is much that I want to tell him about Jesus. And, he will have much to tell me, of that I am sure.

> *"I love them that love me; and those that seek me early shall find me."*
>
> ***Proverbs 8:17*** (KJV)

Christian was christened as an infant in the same Greek Orthodox Church as his father and his uncle John. And for the record, I had no part in naming him... just so you know. I believe and declare that God has very special plans for my grandson. After all:

Christian is the third generation of firstborn males.

Christian is the fifth generation of believers in Jesus Christ as the Son of God.

Christian is the fifth generation (that I am aware of) to be blessed with the legacy of faith in and love for our Savior, Christ Jesus; which entitles him to all the promises of God as a child of God.

> *"And if children, then heirs; heirs of God, and joint-heirs with Christ:"*
>
> ***Romans 8:17*** (KJV)

EPILOGUE

...

As I end this book, the COVID-19 virus has emerged and has become a pandemic! Now, more than ever, we need Jesus! We need to call upon His Name for help and healing for the whole world! Most of all, we need His peace, the inner peace that only He can give us! My heart and prayers go out to all the victims and their families, all over the world! We will get through this with the grace of God! The following are but a fraction of some of my favorite facts found in the Bible. I pray you keep them in your heart. If I did not use them in this book, I did use them in my other book, AGAPE.

- God is love, (1 John 4:8 & 4:16)
- God has a plan for your life, (Jeremiah 29:11)
- Seek Jesus, He won't refuse you, (John 6:37)
- Jesus is the only way to Father God, (John 14:6)
- Your name is in Jesus' scars, (Isaiah 49:16)
- Speak Faith to our children, (Romans 10:17)
- We must arm ourselves against evil with the full armour of God! (Ephesians 6:11-17)

We are all loved equally by Father God and Jesus! Do not let anyone tell you that you are unworthy, unloved or unwanted. God Himself calls you worthy, He chose you because He loves you. Jesus died for you because He loves you! And do not ever forget, we must tell our children, so they do not believe in the lies of the thief, Satan. Remember, the thief *"comes to steal, to kill, and to destroy"*. (John 10:10)

Please keep in mind, the promises of God that were spoken over the children of Israel apply to non-Jewish people as well because we have been adopted through Jesus Christ. Through our LORD and Savior, Jesus Christ, we too are children of God and are entitled to all the promises found in His Holy Word!

The longer you wait, the more of His awesome blessings you are missing out on! And the longer you wait, the more chances you miss to pass your legacy of faith and love for Jesus Christ as your savior to your future generations. If not from you, who then will tell them the truth that is written in <u>The HOLY BIBLE</u>, which is God's Word?

Please remember to express your love to your children not only with hugs and kisses, but tell them and tell them often. Introduce them to Jesus early. In doing so, you are planting seeds for generations to come. We *must not turn a blind eye out of love nor out of ignorance and allow our children to go their own way without guidance. If we do we are leaving them wide open to be manipulated by the devil! And if we do that, we have failed them! We must not spoil our children and grandchildren to the point of losing their souls!*
Nanette Crapo 03/28/2020

> **"...For we wrestle not against flesh and blood, but against principalities, against powers, against the rulers of the darkness of this world, against spiritual wickedness in high places."**

> *<u>Ephesians 6:12</u>* (KJV)

ADDENDUM
03/30/2020
COVID-19 PANDEMIC

*"Through the tender mercy of our God,
With which the Dayspring from
on high has visited us;
To give light to those who sit in darkness
and the shadow of death,
To guide our feet into the way of peace."*

Luke 1:78-79 (NKJV)

*"In Him was life, and the life was the
light of men.
And the light shine in the darkness, and
the darkness did not comprehend it."*

John 1:4-5 (NKJV)

Jesus *is* the Eternal Life and Light that overshadows the darkness. As I sit here in my room, I am very aware that many people are sitting alone in the darkness in fear of the COVID-19 pandemic. Tomorrow is Easter Sunday and churches have to limit the number of their congregations or have services on-line. Hospitals are full to capacity and thousands are ill, many have lost their lives. There is a plague of locus in Africa. The economy has all but shut down with millions out of work. Fear has gripped the whole world. I encourage everyone to turn to Jesus for hope, courage and peace. I would like to end this book with the following verses from Psalms. I would also like to encourage everyone to do as Jesus instructed me to do when I was in my darkest hour... *"Read Psalms."* *(Read the whole book of Psalms, not just Psalm 23.)*

> **"Yes, though I walk through the**
> **valley of the shadow of death,**
> **I will fear no evil;**
> **For You are with me;**
> **Your rod and Your staff, they comfort me."**

Psalm 23:4 (NKJV)

> **"No evil shall befall you,**
> **Nor shall any plague come near**
> **your dwelling;**
> **For He shall give His angels charge over you,**
> **To keep you in all your ways.**

Psalm 91:10-11 (NKJV)

> **"I shall not die, but live,**
> **And declare the works of the LORD."**

Psalm 117:17 (NKJV)

> **"Blessed is the nation whose God is**
> **the LORD;"**

Psalm 33:12 (NKJV)

May God bless each and every one of you in this our hour of need!
Nanette Crapo 03/30/2020

Jesus said:

"Peace I leave with you. My peace I give to you; not as the world gives do I give to you. Let not your heart be troubled, neither let it be afraid."

John 14:27 (NKJV)

"And this is the promise that He has promised us -- eternal life."

1 John 2:25 (NKJV)

ACKNOWLEDGEMENTS

• • •

This book was inspired by my sons, John N. Karamitsos and Anastasios (Tasos) K. Karamitsos II. They both have encouraged me to tell my story, my testimony. I have also been inspired by my only grandchild, Christian Alexander Karamitsos, the firstborn son of my firstborn son, Tasos.

Special acknowledgment to all that have contributed to this book; either with special knowledge of, or as witnesses to some of my stories. I appreciate all their cooperation and collaboration that has enabled this book to come to fruition. They are listed in alphabetical order as per their first names:

Anastasios K. Karamitsos II
(Angels and the Toy Car) (Superman....at the Parthenon
(Up, Up And Away...!) (Holy Spirit and a 9 mm Screw)

Christian A. Karamitsos
(A Boy Named Christian)

Dimitris Chrysafis of Athens, Greece:
(Superman and the Superhero at the Parthenon)

John N. Karamitsos

(Up, Up And Away! Superman Flies Again) (Angels On Vacation) (Holy Spirit vs 22 Slug)

Lisa A. Rachel Crapo
(Legacy of a Mother's Faith and Love) (Holy Spirit vs The Gas Leak)

Mark E. Curry
(Legacy of a Mother's Faith and Love)

Max J. Crapo
(Legacy of a Mother's Faith and Love) (The Night Holy Spirit Screamed) (Holy Spirit vs the Gas Leak)

Patti T. of Sour Lake, Texas:
(Shadow People)

Phyllis J. Cusher
(Heart of Innocence) (Fruit Of The Spirit)

Sharon Crapo Curry Chrysafis of Athens, Greece:
(Peaceful Sleep of a Child) (Legacy of a Mother's Faith and Love) (Doubting Thomas) (Holy Spirit vs the Gas Leak)

Sotiris Chrysafis of Athens, Greece:
(Holy Spirit vs The Gas Leak) (Christening and Baptism)

REFERENCES

...

HOLY BIBLE, CONCORDANCE (KJV)
RED LETTER EDITION, King James Version
TRANSLATED OUT OF THE ORIGINAL TONGUES AND WITH THE FORMER TRANSLATIONS DILIGENTLY COMPARED AND REVISED. AUTHORIZED KING JAMES VERSION. THE WORLD PUBLISHING COMPANY. CLEVELAND AND NEW YORK
PUBLISHED BY THE WORLD PUBLISHING COMPANY 2231 WEST 110TH STREET
CLEVELAND 2 – OHIO
MANUFACTURED IN THE UNITED STATES OF AMERICA

THE HOLY BIBLE, NEW KING JAMES VERSION (NKJV)
Scripture taken from the NEW KING JAMES VERSION. Copyright 1982 by Thomas Nelson. Used by permission. All rights reserved.

THE HOLY BIBLE, NEW INTERNATIONAL VERSION (NIV)
Scripture quotations taken from THE HOLY BIBLE, NEW INTERNATIONAL VERSION, NIV. Copyright 1973, 1978, 1984,2011 by Biblica, Inc.

Personal Journals of Nanette Crapo, Author